GROW ORGANIC
SALAD LEAVES
AND GREENS

GROW ORGANIC
SALAD LEAVES AND GREENS

INDOORS OR OUTDOORS, ALL YEAR ROUND

CHARLES DOWDING

Previously published in 2018 as *Salad Leaves for all Seasons* by

Green Books
An imprint of UIT Cambridge Ltd
www.greenbooks.co.uk

PO Box 145, Cambridge CB4 1GQ, England
+44 (0)1223 302 041

First edition published in 2008

Charles Dowding has asserted his moral rights under the
Copyright, Designs and Patents Act 1988.

Front cover photograph by Cora Mueller / Shutterstock.com.
Back cover photographs by Steph Hafferty and Edward Dowding.

All interior photographs, with the exception of those listed below, are by the
author, Steph Hafferty and Edward Dowding.
Page 1: Josh Rogers.
Pages 33, 107: Finn McAteer.

Design by Jayne Jones

ISBN: 9780857845542 (paperback)
ISBN: 9780857845559 (ebook)
Also available for Kindle

Disclaimer: The advice herein is believed to be correct at
the time of printing, but the author and publisher accept
no liability for actions inspired by this book.

ep-3-1

ACKNOWLEDGEMENTS

To all the people who have helped me grow
vegetables over the years, especially:

Victor Crutchley, David Sanders and Bepp, Lisa, Brian,
Anne, Pippa Beckett, David Godfrey, Wallee McDonnell,
Susie Corbett, Bill Craster, Sara Frears, Paul and Ulli
from Germany, Hilda Denham, Nicky Hembridge,
Vicky Matthews, Finny Fox-Davies, Kate Plowman,
Greg Morter, Nicole Leathley, Heather Mora, Emily Evans,
Geoff Branson, Rosie Stott, Alex Simon, Darren McGrath,
Mick Denney, Felix Hofmann, Finn McAteer,
Lara Honnor, Josh Rogers.
And special thanks to Stephanie Hafferty.

CONTENTS

INTRODUCTION

Since starting vegetable growing in 1981, I have become more and more fascinated by salad. Lettuce was one of the first crops in 1983, from my newly created acre and a half of raised beds in the old farm orchard. In May and June of that year I sold many dozens of butterhead lettuce hearts, some in the village, where a surprised neighbour commented that there was enough flavour for her not to need any mayonnaise!

That set me wondering; where had the flavour gone in other lettuce? All I had done was to grow them in honest soil to organic standards. Over the next few years, lettuce became one of my bestsellers and also, luckily, one of the few slightly profitable crops to grow – partly because it matured so quickly, and partly because it always sold so well, in spite of the little grey slugs lurking inside many hearts (as they do…). But in those days, other salad leaves were not in demand and lamb's lettuce was almost the only different kind I grew, mostly to sell in March and April.

Moving to France in 1991 helped me to explore some new possibilities. Oddly enough the kitchen garden at our small farm grew purslane as one of its main summer weeds, far more than we could eat. Endives were often sold in local markets and pretty oak-leaved lettuce as well, but even there the locals' phrase *une salade* meant lettuce or endive heart only. There was no interest in loose leaves of rocket, which after all came from Italy, or in oriental leaves from even farther away.

So my interest in the great potential of salad leaves lay dormant for a while. After returning to Britain, it was a request from Bill the Butcher in Bruton to create some bags of mixed leaves that opened my eyes to the possibilities for anyone with some soil, compost, a bit of spare room in the garden and a spirit of adventure. Since then I have enjoyed experimenting with different seeds, sowing dates, picking methods and growing media to discover new flavours, shapes and colours at all different times of year.

Salad bags from Lower Farm are now sold in many outlets within about four miles, enough distance to provide enough customers for everything I can grow. Picking takes much more time than growing and is a demanding job, bent over in the cool of the dawn; two of us gather leaves before and just after breakfast then mix, wash and pack them immediately so that people can eat them that day or pubs can serve them for lunch. Customer feedback is enthusiastic, often emphasising the leaves' flavour and keeping ability – which is because they are healthy and alive.

In this book I offer you the information needed to grow and harvest leaves of a similar quality and variety.

Leaf lettuce, coriander flowers and peas for shoots.

The Conjuror's Hat

Salad leaves are one of the quickest and easiest vegetables you can grow. More than that, plants that are well looked after will provide long successions of harvests, without having to repeatedly sow or plant again. How to continually crop the same plants and give them a surprisingly long life – a main theme of this book – is explained in Part One. New leaves just keep appearing – it is almost magical.

Another key theme in the book is growing in small spaces and containers, which can be impressively productive. You may also find yourself appreciating the growing beauty of your range of salad plants, as much as their abundant contributions to the table.

The leaves you pick will also be full of seasonal characteristics, reflecting how different salads give of their best at particular times of year. Appreciating this calendar of salad seasons, explained in Part Two, will help towards more success in growing healthy plants. In Part Three I offer a tour of the great range of salad possibilities, and all necessary information on how to obtain the best from them. Lastly, in Part Four there is an explanation of how to use covered spaces to extend the season of growth and to ensure a steady supply of leaves for much of the winter, as well as earlier outdoor harvests in the spring.

Charles Dowding, Homeacres

PART ONE
GROWING
LEAVES

CHAPTER ONE

HIGH YIELDS, SMALL SPACES, SPECIAL METHODS

LEARNING NEW TRICKS

You do not need a large garden to grow good amounts of leaves. Small beds or containers can produce surprisingly large harvests. Whatever the size of your growing area, the important thing is to make the most of it.

Salad leaves are a great starting point if you have not grown food before. They reach harvest rapidly, look attractive while growing and bring a sparkle to many meals, with almost no preparation time.

KEYS TO SUCCESS

Salad plants can be long-lived when they are correctly chosen for the season and well tended. This is a key aspect of successful growing, enabling you to enjoy high production from small areas. Which plants are grown and how they are picked is as important as your general sowing and growing techniques (see Chapter 2 for more details). Careful choosing and tending of plants makes even containers and window boxes capable of producing enough leaves to be highly worthwhile over a long period.

Charles picking salad for sale at Homeacres in spring.

I share many tips about sowing at the best moment for each salad plant. The season, the moon and the weather all play a part, and growing your own food helps you to be aware of important natural rhythms. This is empowering knowledge which brings health, not least from having more leaves to eat.

FIRST STEPS

Keep your initial purchases small and simple. Catalogues and shops are full of expensive accessories that are not necessary. The main things you need are seed and/or plants, a container or bed to grow them in, some good compost, a watering can and, above all, sufficient time to tend your plants on a regular basis. Once a growing space is set up, the main work of salad growing is to pick the leaves.

Start in a small way, but also experiment with lots of different salad plants to see which ones grow best for you and provide leaves which you enjoy eating. Soon you will get the hang of managing an interesting range of plants at different times of year to keep those healthy harvests coming.

LARGER SPACES

If there is room outside and you want plenty of leaves, think about a bed along the lines of those in Chapter 3, which measure 1.2x2.4m (4x8'). Over a trial season, these produced weekly harvests of around 1-2kg (2-4lb) of mixed leaves between late April and mid-October, then rather less until Christmas.

Once the materials are sourced, you can assemble new beds rapidly and in almost any location – on top of grass, gravel or paved areas. An open space is better than against a wall, because more light will give better growth.

In view of the productivity of well-tended salad plants, my advice to anyone with a large garden is to scale down their salad area and manage it more tightly. Valuable compost is then concentrated on a smaller space and there is less weeding and watering.

Larger beds are useful for those plants needing room to grow, such as the wide range of hearting plants. Study the book and plan a growing space to be in line with your intended harvests.

You can keep one bed fully productive throughout a growing season by resowing or replanting as soon as gaps appear. Check the information in Part Two, Chapter 9, to see which plants are coming into their period of most productive and healthy growth, according to the time of year.

SMALLER SPACES

Small spaces can profit from the use of large containers, which may even be quite shallow for salad, as long as they are well watered in dry weather. The large round lettuce pot in Chapter 4, page 45, which yields leaves for three months off a dozen plants, has a diameter of 63cm (25"), a depth of 22cm (9") and contains about 40 litres of compost. Or look at the recycled plastic window boxes, which measure 100x 20cm and are 15cm deep (39x8x6"). They hold 15 litres of compost and offer worthwhile yields of leaves for a long

Fleece is so useful over early plantings. In late April it's still cold but seedlings are well established under fleece.

The same view 19 days later, after the fleece has been removed. Vegetables are now growing strongly.

period (see Chapter 4, pages 44-45).

The small volumes of such containers compared with gardens and raised beds means you must fill them with good-quality compost, both to retain as much moisture as possible and to provide nutrients for steady and significant growth. Organic composts are available to meet these criteria (see Resources) and I feel they are the best option for achieving well-balanced, even growth and for highly nutritious leaves. Their nutrient levels can be topped up between crops with, for example, a few handfuls of comfrey and lucerne pellets, to avoid having to refill containers with new compost after every harvest.

SALAD SEASONS

Growing plants in their right season will give you far more success than if you sow anything you fancy at a random time of year. For example, pea shoots and lettuce grow best in the spring, purslane and basil require summer heat, endives and mizuna thrive in autumn, lamb's lettuce (corn salad) and winter purslane in winter.

A seasonal approach achieves more abundant harvests for less time needed. Leaves are healthier too, because insects that live off certain plants are only prevalent at certain times: avoid growing them in those periods and growth will be healthier.

An extra benefit of this approach is the constantly changing nature of your harvests. Salad is not the same old thing, day in day out, for months on end. April's leaves are quite different from August's, while many leaves in a bowl of late autumn salad, for example, are quite peculiar to that season and are suited to boosting your health as winter approaches.

FLAVOUR

With the changing seasons come frequent and fascinating changes in leaf flavour. I have devoted a whole chapter to this subject, to whet your appetite and illustrate the surprisingly large range of tastes to be had in a bowl of leaves.

THE BENEFITS OF ORGANIC GROWING

The main benefit in growing your own leaves is that they are eaten fresh, firm and full of flavour. Organic methods help to achieve this: firstly from healthier plants, whose growth is easier to manage, and secondly by nourishing you and your family and friends with extra-nutritious food. I outline ways of constructing or assembling beds of any size that are full of compost mostly, perhaps some soil, plus a few additions for extra trace elements.

Growing plants organically and in their right season means that pests are mostly absent. Occasionally aphids congregate in the spring, before ladybirds arrive to eat them, and they can simply be washed off after picking the leaves. Slugs are more problematic in certain situations, such as enclosed yards with many walls, and I offer ideas for dealing with them. Pests and disease will always be with us, so we need to work out the best way of minimizing their impact.

A selection of December salad leaves, mostly grown in the polytunnel.

Best results are from understanding how they operate and gardening accordingly, rather than gardening in a random way and having to deal with unexpected problems that arise.

THE MOON AND UNSEEN INFLUENCES

Earthly influences are powerful, so sowing dates are governed firstly by the season and secondly by the weather.

Yet salad leaves are nearly all water, and water is massively influenced by the moon, suggesting that salad leaves grown according to the moon's phases will grow more strongly (see Chapter 7).

QUALITY LEAVES, FULL OF FLAVOUR

Quality is the main reason for growing your own leaves. They will be different from most of those for sale, much livelier, brighter, crisper, more colourful and with exciting tastes to enjoy. You can create your own palette of salad flavours – have a look at Chapter 5 and choose from its wide-ranging and amazingly long menu, and then use Chapter 10 to inspire you with ideas for eating them.

CHAPTER TWO

VITAL KNOWLEDGE FOR SUCCESSFUL HARVESTS

LESS SOWING, MORE PICKING

Brief summary

* Sow seeds thinly for picking individual leaves, more thickly for cutting rows or clumps.
* Wider spacings give healthier leaves over a longer time.
* Grow in best-quality compost, or surface-dress garden soil with good compost.
* For picking you can choose to cut baby leaves or pick medium-sized ones, depending on salad type and your preferences.
* Harvested leaves will keep for days if cool and moist.
* One sowing for each season can be enough to have leaves all year round (fewer in winter).

Late summer, two days after interplanting spinach, salad rocket and Chinese cabbage between lettuce still cropping.

HOW TO SOW SEEDS

The two main choices are between sowing directly into beds or containers, or sowing into modules or seed trays on a window sill, conservatory or greenhouse bench (see Chapter 6). Direct outdoor sowings are harder to space thinly and tend to emerge as dense rows of seedlings, which then do best if thinned out. Module-sown seed is easier to ration out, from one seed per module for lettuce, to two or three for spinach, mustards and other salads. A third possibility is thick sowings into seed trays or boxes, usually indoors, to have crops of 'micro leaves' cut as seedlings or picked as baby leaves for pretty garnishes (see Chapter 4, pages 47-49).

Always sow into well-dampened and fine-textured soil or compost. Salad seed is mostly small, so it is best sown shallow – half a centimetre deep and less in the case of lettuce. Deeper sowings usually take longer to emerge and may not come up at all. Seedbeds need to be damp for just a few days until seed is germinated: in dull, cool conditions this means no watering at all between sowing and the appearance of seedlings.

In sunny weather, water daily with a fine rose. You want the surface to dry in between waterings, because that offers less encouragement to slugs, mildew and weed seeds.

HOW TO PLANT

Planting is not sowing, which happens to seeds. It's taking a plant you sowed, say, three to four weeks ago and setting it into a hole in the ground. The ground may be compost or soil, whatever is the surface layer of your beds. In hot climates there may be a mulch of grass or straw, but in damp climates such as the UK, compost is the best mulch.

So to plant, you make a hole slightly bigger and deeper than the seedling's rootball, put the plant in place, push firm and make sure the plant's stem is all buried. This makes for strong and stable plants! Also they stay moist for longer, especially because every time you plant, unless it's raining, you drop some water directly on the rootball. Not only to give moisture, but to help the plant root settle in contact with soil and compost.

Lettuce *Grenoble Red*, nearly nine months old, picked regularly and given no feeds.

After planting, there is a lull of no growth while the settling-in process happens. Plants are vulnerable to pests at this stage, so check for slugs at dusk and cover with fleece if rabbits may be around.

HOW TO INTERPLANT

This sounds more difficult than it is, and gives a lot of fun, plus the satisfaction of making more of scarce resources, namely time and space. You pop plants between other plants that have grown a while and will soon finish. While the new plants are settling, the old ones are winding down towards a final harvest – say in two to four weeks time. The photos explain this nicely and you can see how pretty it looks.

SPACING PLANTS FOR DIFFERENT HARVESTS

Many salad plants grow large if given space, and large leaves are quick to pick. Well-spaced plants that are regularly picked can crop for long periods of up to three months, depending on the time of year. Larger leaves have a different flavour from baby leaves and a firmer texture, which helps them to keep well after harvest.

Thicker sowings are suitable for cutting lots of baby leaves, but crop for a shorter period. Cutting leaves therefore means you need to resow more often, to have a continuity of salad, compared with thinner sowings that you pick.

Try some different methods and find the system of growing and cropping which best suits your taste, lifestyle

Autumn brassicas intersown on the diagonal between lettuce.

and garden. I have tried many methods over the decades and have enjoyed most success with a combination of three aspects of growing, two of which are intimately related to plant spacing:

* **Widely spaced plants,** 20-25cm (8-10") apart in all directions, enables plants to live longer, develop more leaf colour, and makes picking easier. Spacing any wider gives no added benefit for salad leaves and also results in an increased growth of weeds, plus a need for extra water. Most effective use of space is made by planting 'on the square'. Imagine a grid of squares across your planting area: plant at all the corners as well as into the centre of every square to achieve an equal distance between plants in every direction (see right).

* **Picking a few of the outer leaves of all plants on a regular basis,** rather than cutting across the top of them, ensures a steady supply of leaves. A further benefit is that plants live longer, through careful handling and never having their small, central leaves cut. These do most of the photosynthesis and enable new growth to continue for several weeks, with plants in a state of suspended adolescence.

* **Sowing or planting into well-composted soil.** Over a long period, compost provides steady moisture and temperature, and sufficient nutrients as plants require them. Salad plants are not normally considered 'heavy feeders' – unlike, say, tomatoes. However their growth is constant and is well adapted to the nutrients, water and energy that a good compost provides.

GATHERING LEAVES

New growth is powered by the small, central leaves. At the other extreme, older leaves continue enlarging until they mature, at a size dictated by the distance from other plants, and according to the time of year.

Planting into the grid pattern

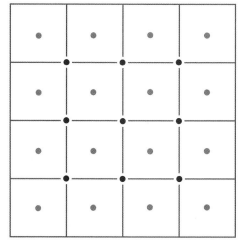

● Planting into the intersect
● Planting into the centre of every square

The best quality and most viable leaves are those in between the baby ones at the centre and the large, mature, sometimes yellowing, diseased and slug-eaten ones at the edge. Keep picking the adolescent leaves, at intervals of three to five days in summer to a fortnight in winter, so that plants just keep on growing. Besides the advantage of having less sowing and replanting to do, there will be fewer pests and healthier leaves, because you are always picking them before they reach their time of decay, so there is less food and habitat for pest and disease.

Salad boxes before the 13th harvest.
Yield to date 2.32kg (5lb) without feeds.

Baby leaves are more tender but are fiddly to pick individually and are usually harvested by cutting rows of thickly sown seedlings. When doing this, it is difficult to avoid the presence of some yellowing and mildew-infected leaves which occur in densely sown rows, and cutting must be at a height that does not destroy the growing points of the smallest leaves. When using this method, I have found that most plants live for less long, especially lettuce.

A third possibility in larger gardens is to have rows with about 7-8cm between plants, and 30-40cm between rows (3x15"). The extra spacing allows for repeat cuttings of somewhat larger leaves, as well as allowing better longevity of certain salads such as rocket, chard and mizuna.

STORING AND REVIVING LEAVES

Leaves grown in healthy, fertile soil or compost, and carefully picked when moist, keep remarkably well in cool, damp conditions, such as in a polythene bag at the bottom of the fridge. Basically, they stay alive. A temperature of 5-7°C (41-45°F) is ideal for preserving well-grown leaves in good condition for up to a week if need be. Just be sure to bag up only top-quality leaves with no yellowing or mildew.

Should you pick dry, limp leaves – say, on a warm afternoon – place them immediately in cold water so that they can soak up moisture and become firm again. Water is the basis of everything and leaves are nothing without it.

LETTUCE

Until recently lettuce was often the only salad leaf eaten in Britain, and was usually grown into fine, dense hearts. Now we can buy seeds of many other leaves, but lettuce is often still the mainstay of salads because of an increasing range of attractive varieties available, and because of its productivity, especially when the outer leaves are repeatedly picked off. Such treatment can keep a window box or container in production for two to three months at a time from the same plants, with a few leaves at each picking. The first leaves are always a little tricky because they lie close to the soil or compost. Be gentle with the plant at this stage, since it is so young and tender. Then each successive picking becomes easier as the lettuce stem gradually thickens and elongates above soil level, like a stumpy little tree.

Finally, after up to three months (or much longer for lettuce which have been overwintered under cover), the squat stem will stretch upwards and become a flower stem, at which point its leaves become small and bitter. Twist rather than pull out the plant (it's good to leave small roots in the soil as food for microbes) and replace with something different, such as rocket or spinach.

Using this method of picking will provide an even supply of leaves over long periods. Nearly all salad plants can be continually cropped like this and a nice benefit is that they grow faster in hot weather, just when you feel like eating more salad. You also need to think ahead and have young plants ready for when existing batches finally rise to seed. A second bed, container or space of some kind is useful for growing on the next batch of plants.

SALAD DAYS FOREVER, IN DIFFERENT SEASONS

For salad days which go on and on:
* Start in late winter or early spring with lettuce, spinach, chard, peas and some herbs, most of which will crop until July.
* Make another sowing in late May, to take over from the first batch in early July. The second sowing can be a mixture of lettuce, chard, summer purslane, basil, and the odd endive.
* In mid-July, sow more lettuce and an autumn selection of endives, chicories, rocket, and various herbs.
* Lastly in late August sow the winter range of rocket, chicories, hardy lettuce, winter purslane, land cress and oriental leaves. See Part Two, Chapter 9 for more details.

Timing of sowings is important in late summer – see later chapters to find precise dates for each kind of leaf. A surprisingly large range of plants lend themselves to production of leaves in the winter season. Although growth is slower and harvests are smaller, flavours are more intense and the pleasure of having your own leaves when they are so rare is a great bonus in itself, apart from the delight of eating them.

SALAD ROTATION

This is not about spinning water out of leaves, but about growing salad of different plant groups in turn, so that

Rocket interplanted with lettuce *Bijou* in September.

October interplanting of endive between lettuce that has perhaps one more week of harvest.

Before and after (front) harvesting a week's growth of lettuce in June.

Chapter 4) and herbs and flowers, and by following the tips in this book, you should be able to keep growing healthy leaves.

Plant families of salad leaves

Apiaceae/Umbelliferae: carrot, chervil, coriander, dill, fennel, mibuna, parsley, sweet cicely
Asteraceae/Compositae: chicory, endive, lettuce
Brassicaceae/Cruciferae: Chinese cabbage, kale, kohlrabi, land cress, mibuna, mizuna, mustard, pak choi, radish, rape, rocket, tatsoi, turnip, watercress
Chenopodiaceae: beetroot, chard, orache, spinach
Fabaceae/Leguminosae: broad bean, pea
Lamiaceae: basil, mint, savory
Liliaceae: asparagus, chives, garlic, spring onion
Polygonaceae: sorrel
Portulacaceae: purslane
Rosaceae: salad burnet
Valerianaceae: lamb's lettuce (corn salad)

different pests and diseases have less chance to accumulate in soil, compost and containers. Lettuce, endive and chicory are all closely related, so when they finish it is a good idea to grow any of the brassicas, beet family or herbs and flowers next. Look at the list of plant families below so that, when you have enough space, perhaps half a year can elapse before members of the same family are grown in the same spot.

Sometimes rotation of crops is not possible, especially where you are filling a restricted area with many kinds of leaf. In small beds or containers it can be more feasible to mix plants up together rather than worry about rotating them in sections. By growing a wide variety of leaves from all families, together with some other vegetables such as baby carrots and beetroot (see

Rotation of salads with other vegetables

The advice on rotation above and in this book generally assumes that salad is the reader's principal and perhaps only vegetable crop.

However, although many vegetables grow too large for the confined spaces covered here, there are some which can be grown in small spaces, before or after crops of salad leaves. I list a few

In the same plant family – salad rocket and savoy cabbage.

here to give you some ideas: they all grow in half a season, allowing the other half for growing salad.

As an example, you could sow lettuce in late March to harvest through May and June, then grow beetroot as the second crop (see below). Or grow early carrots as below, then plant chicories and endives in late July and up to mid-August, for harvesting in October and November. The first crop can have more time to mature if you raise plants of the second harvest in pots or modules, where they can grow for a month or so before being set in their final position.

* **Beetroot:** sow March–early April, harvest July, or sow early July, harvest October onwards

* **Calabrese:** sow March (indoors), plant April, harvest July
* **Carrots:** sow March, harvest June–July; or sow July, harvest October–November
* **Fennel, bulb:** sow July, harvest September–November
* **French beans:** sow early July, harvest September–October
* **Leeks, baby:** sow early April, harvest July; or sow July, harvest winter
* **Onions:** plant late March, harvest July
* **Radish:** sow March–April, harvest May–June; or sow late July–August, harvest September–November
* **Turnips,** sow early August for autumn harvest – tasty leaves as well

CHAPTER THREE

SOWING, PLANTING, AND HARVESTING THROUGH THE YEAR

AN EXPERIMENT WITH SALAD BEDS

Brief summary

* New beds can be placed on existing surfaces, with no previous preparation. Check below for one or two exceptions.

* Grass is fine for a base and does not need to be dug or turned over.

* Sides of 15cm (6") or more can be of wood or plastic: both have advantages and disadvantages.

* Fill beds with compost, soil and manure according to what is locally available.

* A range of different plants can be sown or planted to give a continuous and varied mix of leaves.

* Use the information in other chapters to decide what you will sow and plant at different times of year.

* Beds will need regular watering in dry seasons and slug control in wet ones.

* The main season of harvest is late April to October. Outside this period, leaves grow more slowly.

* 2-3cm (an inch or so) of fresh compost on top annually will maintain health and fertility.

A new bed of compost on grass in October,
planted with salads for winter, then meshed over.

A SALAD EXPERIMENT

First off, I created two new beds in late February, one on gravel and one on grass. In both instances there was no work on the existing ground surface. I simply created a framework and filled it with organic matter, then sowed and planted straightaway. Plants were picked over and looked after as previously described and yielded leaves over long periods. When each harvest was finished, I sowed or planted again with different ones as the seasons changed.

By following the descriptions of what happened in these beds, you will better appreciate the possibilities available and how much time and effort may be needed. Then at the chapter's end is a table of the weekly yields I obtained, from which you can work out how much space you need in relation to the size of beds I used.

ASSEMBLING NEW BEDS

The beds were made from old decking wood of 2.4m (8') lengths, three pieces per bed. One was cut in half to make the ends of 1.2m (4') and I joined the four corners with angle braces, screwed to the insides of the ends of the planks.

In this particular case I sought to recycle some wood, trusting that preservatives will not seep into the soil, and there is limited information about this. There are other ways of creating beds with untreated wood: for example, some other beds I made were of new softwood, which I brushed with two coats of Osmo Wood Protector, a biocide-free oil. This is fine for soil organ-

isms, but the wood still decayed within six years.

Another idea is to buy a kit of green plastic sides, made from recycled PVC. The strips contain air, making them effectively 'double-glazed' and able to better regulate temperature extremes in the beds – cooler in summer and warmer in winter. Plastic is less sturdy than wood but quick to assemble. For any bed you can anchor the middle of each side, to prevent bowing outwards, by driving a peg into the ground where it is soft enough.

FILLING NEW BEDS

* To fill the enclosures I used what came to hand, starting with 5cm (2") of the neighbour's reasonably well-rotted horse manure on top of the yard gravel for one bed, and on grass for the other. I made a small ramp so that two large wheelbarrow loads could be tipped straight into each bed. Old manure is basically compost: it holds moisture and slowly releases nutrients as plants require them.

* After levelling off, I emptied five wheelbarrow loads of compost made from garden recycled waste into each bed, which more than filled them – some treading down was required. This compost had passed through a 10mm ($^1/_2$") sieve before delivery, to remove any wood and plastic. Compost is often offered from a 15mm ($^3/_4$") sieve, which is OK but means more plastic. Do avoid a sieving of 25mm (1"), which would mean large pieces of wood and waste materials.

* Then I spread about 10kg (22lb) of basalt (volcanic) rock dust (see

A bed planted with winter salads for autumn – see the sequel on page 35.

Resources) over each bed, my hunch being that this ensures good levels of trace elements in growing plants. It breaks down slowly over many years.

* Lastly I spread one sack of organic multipurpose compost on top to ensure sufficient nutrients, since, in spite of sieving, the recycled compost contains quite large amounts of tiny pieces of wood, which can absorb nutrients as they continue to decompose. Salads are not heavy feeders but they do need a regular supply of many nutrients.

* The cost of these ingredients was about £11 per bed plus two hours of my time to fetch and spread them. Every household will have different possibilities but the principle of some animal manure on the bottom and finer compost on top is worth aiming for.

* Final smoothing of the compost was with a small plank of plywood, to make the surface even and easier for sowing/planting.

* A final touch was to cover the beds with netting to prevent fouling by cats, until plants were established in mid-April.

SOWING, PLANTING AND CROPPING THE BEDS

The beds were finished by late February, too early for first sowings and plantings, but they were ready to use as soon as the weather turned less cold. March was mild and on the 10th I planted some module-grown lettuce, spinach, chard and coriander, which had been sown six weeks earlier in the greenhouse, and I sowed more of the same directly in the surface of the beds, as well as some peas.

A week later I set out plants of komatsuna, turnip greens, ruby mustard and rocket. These are marginal for spring use because their leaves are often holed by flea beetles and they crop for only a short time before flowering – the plants in this case were finished by early May. However, any salad in early spring is welcome and they bring different flavours.

The real stars in spring salads are lettuce, the main ingredient of my first harvest on 14 April, which weighed in at 0.5kg (1lb) per bed. By the following week the quantity had doubled and it stayed thereabouts until early June. The range of ingredients reflected my initial sowings, and lettuce comprised about three quarters of the total.

I continued with occasional sowings until late summer, to keep the beds always full after clearing old plants. The table on page 34 lists all sowings and planting for a whole season's cropping and is to give you ideas; bear in mind that it covers both beds and so half the plantings and clearings would be needed for just one bed.

Pick leaves when it is convenient for you: every day, twice weekly or weekly, although any longer than weekly will see them become large and more dam-aged by pest for disease. When picked damp in the early morning, late evening or after rain, and washed in cold water, leaves remain crisp and firm for many days – say, in a polythene bag kept in the bottom of a fridge.

WATERING

Large volumes of compost can hold plenty of moisture, more than ordinary soil, so a thorough watering once weekly should be sufficient in dry weather. For a bed of 1.2x2.4m (4x8') you will need 30-50 litres (7-11 gallons) of water each time, and every three days or so in the hottest weather. It is better to water gently out of a can with a rose than with a jet of water from a hose, so that water has time to dampen the compost and soak in, rather than running off.

In the summer half of the year, after a few days of sun or warm winds, the sides of raised beds become especially dry and need extra water. Ants often invade any warm, dry spots so it is worth keeping the sides as moist as possible. Recycled plastic is better than wood in this respect.

Mid-October: the frilly mustards (second from front) were the third plantings of the year after spinach, then cucumber.

Charles with a newly planted winter salad bed in October, protected with mesh against rabbits and weather.

SLUGS

Some seasons see enough rain that watering is scarcely necessary, but then slugs require attention instead. On damp evenings from late June to late August, usually after rain, I regularly discovered slugs heading for the salad bed. I have tried many of the more commonly suggested remedies (see Chapter 8, pages 80-82) and find that in seasons of excessive moisture, dusk or dawn patrols to kill them are invaluable.

An advantage of planting at wider spacings and picking leaves regularly is that slugs have less or no hiding place, so there should not be any living on the bed surface. However, expect some slugs when you grow larger, hearting salads.

WEEKLY SOWINGS, PLANTINGS AND CLEARINGS ON BOTH BEDS

The following table is a reflection of my aim to grow many different leaves on two separate beds, to always fill every gap that arose and to keep the beds cropping through winter. It could be simplified by choosing to grow fewer kinds of leaves and leaving occasional bare patches instead.

By using the table for the length of harvest period, and information about different plants in the rest of this book, you can work out roughly what you could be eating when.

I sowed seed into modules in a greenhouse for later planting in the bed, unless the plant name is followed by (s), when it was sown directly into the bed.

Date	Planted	Harvest Period	Remarks
10 Mar	Lettuce, 6 varieties*	11 Apr–early July	Consistent, bulky harvests
	Spinach, *Tarpy*	14 Apr–19 May	Final large picking to cook
	Spinach, *Regiment*	18 Apr–15 Jun	Smaller picks but longer season
	Chard, ruby and yellow	14 Apr–15 Nov	Flowering stems pinched out
	Beet, *Red Titan*	14 Apr–8 Nov	Small, dense, rich colour
	Coriander, *Confetti*	18 Apr–19 Jun	Flowering by mid-May
	Spinach, *Tetona* (s)	18 Apr–22 Jun	Dark, round leaves
	Chard, ruby and yellow (s)	18 Apr–15 Nov	Almost too productive
	Lettuce, 6 varieties (s)	25 Apr–mid-July	Cut, then massively thinned
	Pea, *Ambassador* (s)	18 Apr–12 July	Fleshiest shoots in May
16 Mar	Komatsuna	18 Apr–8 May	Some slug damage
	Turnip greens	18 Apr–8 May	Aphids and virus in May
	Ruby mustard	25 Apr–8 May	Aphids meant small harvest
	Rocket	18 Apr–15 May	Aphids meant small harvest
22 Mar	Spring onion, *White Lisbon*	28 Apr–19 Jun	Each clump made a bunch
28 Mar	Sorrel, broad-leaved	8 May–6 Dec	Many small, tasty harvests
	Red-ribbed dandelion	8 May–29 Nov	Flowering stems pinched out
1 May	Orach (s)	19 May–11 Jul	Small, dark leaves
19 Jun	Endive, yellow leaf	13 Jul–6 Dec	Pretty leaves every week
	Lettuce, 5 varieties**	13 Jul–21 Sep	Consistent growth
	Parsley, curly and plain	20 Jul–13 Dec	Still healthy at year's end
	Radicchio, *Palla Rossa*	17-29 Aug + Oct	Hearts first then regrowth
	Purslane, green	Failed	Disliked wet summer
27 Jul	Mustards, ruby and golden	10 Aug–15 Nov	For autumn not winter leaves
	Leaf radish	10 Aug–26 Oct	For autumn not winter leaves
	Spinach, *Tetona* (s)	24 Aug–1 Nov	Some slug holes
	Rocket (s)	24 Aug–6 Dec	Variable quality, steady growth
	Mizuna (s)	17 Aug–5 Oct	Rapid to start and to flower
30 Jul	Leaf chicory, 10 varieties***(s)	31 Aug–20 Dec	Leaves smaller by December
8 Aug	Lettuce, 4 varieties****	31 Aug–13 Dec	Grenoble Red lasted longest
	Pak Choi, *Joi Choi*	31 Aug–5 Oct	Many slug holes
31 Aug	Lamb's lettuce, *D'Orlanda*	8 Nov–27 Mar	Small, high quality harvests
7 Sep	Mustard, *Golden Streaks*	5 Oct–6 Dec	Feathery leaves, strong taste
	Tatsoi	5 Oct–8 Nov	Mostly slug-holed
14 Sep	Mizuna	5 Oct–6 Dec	Some fungal diseases later
	Kohlrabi, purple-leaved	19 Oct–20 Dec	Small pickings
	Rocket, salad	5 Oct–20 Dec	Good growth in late autumn
	Lamb's lettuce (s)	5 Feb–mid-Apr	Welcome leaves in late winter

* March lettuce varieties: *Grenoble Red, Bijou, Bergamo, Bridgemere, Catalogna, Mottistone*
** June lettuce varieties: *Foxley, Bridgemere, Chartwell, Mottistone, Redina*
*** July leaf chicories: all those listed on p.98
**** August lettuce varieties: *Grenoble Red, Appleby, Rosemoor, Chartwell*

By 4 June, spinach, spring onions and 5.3kg (11lb 10oz) of lettuce have been harvested from each bed – all from March plantings.

April salads sown in autumn: (from left) lamb's lettuce, rocket, spinach, winter purslane, land cress. See page 31.

WEEKLY TOTAL OF LEAVES (TWO BEDS 1.2x2.4m), AND WEATHER NOTES

I include the notes on weather because it affects speed and quality of growth so much. In Somerset, 2007 was characterized by unusual warmth in spring, unusual rainfall in summer and an unusually fine autumn. All three caused extra salad to grow, as long as slugs were kept under control. So yields might be a little lower in other years.

Date	Amount	Remarks
14 Apr	1.0kg (2lb 3oz)	Mostly lettuce, earlier than usual
21 Apr	2.1kg (4lb 10oz)	Unseasonable warmth, even a few pea shoots
25 Apr	1.9kg (4lb 3oz)	Plenty of chard and coriander
1 May	2.0kg (4lb 6oz)	Still so warm, flea beetle holes in rocket, mustard, turnip greens
8 May	2.3kg (5lb 1oz)	Hot weather, unusually large harvests
15 May	2.2kg (4lb 14oz)	Rain at last
24 May	3.1kg (6lb 13oz)	Leaves increasing in size and thickness, weather cooler
1 Jun	3.9kg (8lb 9oz)	Large harvest, enough for half a dozen hungry households
8 Jun	4.8kg (10lb 9oz)	Serious surplus! Warm, moist weather
15 Jun	4.4kg (9lb 11oz)	Less spinach
22 Jun	3.9kg (8lb 9oz)	Lettuce slowing down with smaller leaves
29 Jun	3.5kg (7lb 11oz)	Thinner pea shoots
6 Jul	2.8kg (6lb 2oz)	Spring flush is over, some lettuce is flowering
13 Jul	3.1kg (6lb 13oz)	Fleshy leaves in damp weather, slug patrols every night
20 Jul	2.5kg (5lb 8oz)	Leaves harvested in torrential rain, good quality, last of early lettuce
27 Jul	2.2kg (4lb 14oz)	Slight lull and no purslane
3 Aug	2.3kg (5lb 1oz)	More sun is helping growth
10 Aug	2.4kg (5lb 4oz)	New lettuce now producing, also mustard and leaf radish
17 Aug	1.9kg (4lb 3oz)	More cool rain, first radicchio heart
24 Aug	1.6kg (3lb 8oz)	Growth slowed by cool, cloudy weather, still squashing slugs
29 Aug	1.9kg (4lb 3oz)	Extra harvest of four radicchio hearts – keep well in fridge
31 Aug	2.5kg (5lb 8oz)	Return of sunshine, healthy lettuce and first chicory leaves
7 Sep	2.3kg (5lb 1oz)	Mix includes lettuce, spinach, rocket, mustards, endive, chicory, sorrel
14 Sep	2.1kg (4lb 10oz)	Leaves still plentiful
21 Sep	1.2kg (2lb 10oz)	Suddenly growth has slowed and some lettuce have flowered
28 Sep	0.4kg (14oz)	Cool autumn mornings, smaller leaves on all plants
5 Oct	1.1kg (2lb 6oz)	Milder weather, a welcome boost to growth
12 Oct	1.1kg (2lb 6oz)	Still a lovely varied mix of many leaves

19 Oct	1.2kg (2lb 10oz)	Warm sun has boosted growth
26 Oct	0.4kg (14oz)	Leaves markedly smaller in reducing daylight
1 Nov	0.4kg (14oz)	Small leaves – still numerous
8 Nov	0.4kg (14oz)	Harvest boosted by the first lamb's lettuce (corn salad)
15 Nov	0.2kg (7oz)	First frost has reduced new growth
22 Nov	0.3kg (10oz)	Small radicchio heart increased the harvest
29 Nov	0.3kg (10oz)	Same as last week, mix of lamb's lettuce, chicories, rocket, bits and pieces
6 Dec	0.4kg (14oz)	Excellent yield after mild weather
13 Dec	0.8kg (1lb 12oz)	Last, large heart of radicchio, beautiful leaves
20 Dec	0.3kg (10oz)	Frosty: Christmas salad of lamb's lettuce, chicory, rocket, chard, mustard

TOTAL 71.2kg (156lb 15oz), equating to 470 salad packs of 150g (5oz), and varied harvests of different flavours every week. Harvests in January and February were about one small meal per week, but by early March I gathered 230g (8oz) of leaves in one harvest, including, leaf chicories and rocket. By early April there was 320g (11oz) per week, including the delicious flowering shoots of mizuna. I cleared the bed at month's end, and spread 5cm (2") of home-made compost. Over the following six weeks I planted it up with beetroot, peas, calabrese and runner beans. Then in late September/October 2008 it was planted again with winter salad – mustards, land cress, lamb's lettuce and mizuna.

These quantities are more than most families or households would require, so you can make smaller beds in proportion to what you eat. But remember that to have enough, you need to grow too much, because growing is affected by unforeseeable events and is not programmable. In times of glut, enjoy giving some fine leaves to friends and neighbours.

Also from late September the weekly harvests are much lower, so at this time of year a larger bed is advantageous. Summer gluts can be avoided by, for example, growing some onions, carrots or early French beans at one end of a large bed. When they finish in early August, there is still time to sow rocket, mustards, kale, chicories, endives, winter purslane, and so forth, to ensure enough leaves when the weather cools down.

Alternatively, take a look at the next chapter for ideas on growing smaller leaves in smaller spaces.

Sowing small seeds in surface compost of a no-dig bed in March.

CHAPTER FOUR

SMALL SPACES AND MICRO LEAVES

GROWING IN CONFINED AREAS AND PICKING BABY LEAVES

Brief summary

* Large containers allow long-term, regular cropping of many leaf types.
* Window boxes are more suited to baby or very small leaves and need more regular watering.
* Growbags are more difficult because they offer sanctuary to slugs.
* Slugs need careful surveillance in container salad growing; I offer tips for reducing their damage, but there are no certain remedies.
* Baby leaves can be grown in trays or beds of shallow compost.

This chapter describes growing salad in containers, window boxes and growbags. It also explains the growing and harvesting of baby salads, sometimes called micro or living leaves.

Lettuce crop well in containers, these have been picked many times already.

SUITABLE CONTAINERS AND WINDOW BOXES

The more compost you can fit in a container, the longer you will be able to crop your salad and the larger the leaves will be. I have had good crops from round terracotta pots of 40-60cm (15-24") diameter, reused plastic mushroom boxes just 10cm (4") deep, and a range of window boxes of different sizes and materials.

A major constraint in container growing is the need to water frequently, so terracotta, which breathes moisture from the compost and out to the atmosphere, is less desirable, though it looks lovely. Glazed pots are better in this respect and you can also line the insides of clay containers with polythene, especially the sides of small terracotta window boxes.

Plastic containers don't have this problem and are lighter to move around. But since plastic conducts heat more quickly than clay, roots may be (though in temperate climates rarely are) damaged by heat in summer and frost in winter. A solution for this is 'double-glazed' recycled plastic window boxes (see Resources), whose layer of air between the PVC sides acts as a heat buffer.

I hesitate to recommend plastic because of its dubious pedigree and afterlife, but sheer durability makes it a reasonably ecological choice, as plastic containers can be re-used so many times. Harvests from plastic containers have always been as good as those from terracotta. Reusing is easy because you do not need to wash or sterilize them before refilling and replanting.

Boxes planted October with lettuce *Grenoble Red* (bottom left), herbs, mustards, salad rocket, plus wild rocket in pots for spring planting. See pages 42-43.

SLUGS

In damp climates, do not underestimate the extent of this problem! One large slug can eat plenty of salad leaves while you are asleep, which is why I recommend pots rather than growbags, whose moist plastic affords a perfect resting place to slugs and snails. Keep growbags for tomatoes and other tall summer crops.

Here are some golden rules for reasonable long-term peace of mind:

* Place containers as far as you can from walls and clumps of thick vegetation, and in as full sunlight as possible.
* Take a wander at dawn and dusk before planting to squash or remove any molluscs.
* Have a rummage under nearby leaves and stones to remove what is lurking.
* Water in the morning so that surface moisture has evaporated by nightfall.

So-called barriers are less effective, worth trying but not guaranteed to be successful. Their limitation is that slugs are only deterred temporarily, rather than reduced in number permanently:

* Copper strips around containers keep most slugs at bay, as long as you ensure there are no leaves overhanging the sides; apparently the copper gives a small electric shock to slimy pests. However, molluscs have been photographed jumping over copper strips!
* Organic slug gel and pellets, salt, soot, wood ash, crushed eggshells, etc. may limit the damage, but are not reliable in some conditions and their overuse may poison the growing medium. Slug nematodes offer protection by poisoning slugs, but only for about six weeks: downsides are that they do not kill snails, and are expensive.

COMPOST

A good compost is the key to abundant, healthy crops. I can offer limited advice here since commercial composts change all the time, especially organic ones that are more difficult to create to a constant formula. Nonetheless I have enjoyed success with West Riding Organics' module compost, (see Resources) which is based on screenings from reservoirs in the Yorkshire Moors. Quality and quantity of growth are excellent. Melcourt make a good

Module plants of spring salads: lettuce, dill, coriander, orache.

February, the same salad boxes after the seventh harvest 230g (8oz) – so 1kg (2lb 3oz) since November.

Another five weeks later, before the 10th harvest of 280g (10 oz) of leaves.

Mid-April, just before picking 280g (10 oz) of leaves – so 2.3kg (3lb) altogether, no feeds.

compost from woody wastes, but it's not organic. I have tried charcoal-based composts with limited success.

PLANT SPACINGS

Salad plants can be grown a little closer in containers than in beds for a greater variety of leaves, as long as they are picked over regularly, which keeps leaf growth in balance with the restricted root runs. If you want fewer and larger leaves, I recommend using the spacings in Part Three.

LIQUID FEEDING (OR NOT) AND REJUVENATING COMPOST

Salad plants are less greedy than tomatoes and you rarely need to feed them.

New compost grows leaves for a few months without extra nutrients. After a crop finishes, one way of rejuvenating compost is to spread some dried comfrey and alfalfa pellets (see Resources) before replanting. Treated in this way, I have containers with three-year-old compost that are still growing healthy plants, which have included tomatoes and courgettes. Or buy a liquid feed to use every two weeks or so.

WATERING

Moisture levels in container compost can be difficult to gauge and in wet weather they can look damp, yet be dry underneath. Remember that plants are pumping moisture from a limited volume: if you are unsure, lift containers to check that they are still reasonably heavy. If using saucers under pots, be careful of waterlogging in wet weather, when it's better to remove them until the sun returns. Also remove saucers in winter.

INFLUENCE OF LIGHT LEVELS

Containers are often placed in part shade, perhaps overlooked by walls, while window boxes, unless they are south-facing, receive only half-light. This makes quite a difference to the vigour of the plants. Choose the sunniest or lightest spot you can find, which helps with slug control as well.

CROPPING EXAMPLES – LEAVES FROM POTS

Below are some examples of salad leaves and vegetables grown by me in containers to illustrate possible sowings, plantings and harvests, as well as what kind of second crops to grow after the first ones finish in midsummer.

All pots and boxes were filled with West Riding Organics' multipurpose compost and no liquid feed was given at all. A little extra compost or nutrients were added before replanting. The only slug defence in a wet summer was regular patrols at dawn and dusk to catch several before damage occurred.

Leaf lettuce and carrots in a large terracotta container

In a round terracotta pot with a diameter of 63cm (25") and a depth of 22cm (9"), holding about 40 litres of compost, I planted 13 lettuce plants on 10 March, from a mid-January indoor sowing. They were *Grenoble Red, Mottistone, Bergamo, Catalogna, Solstice* and *Bridgemere* for a range of leaf shape and colour.

They were picked weekly from mid-April, the leaves about 60 per cent of the size of bed-grown lettuce. The *Solstice* rose to flower in mid-June but the other 12 plants were still producing leaves until late July, making a worthwhile harvest over three and a half months.

To follow them I mixed some alfalfa pellets into the compost and sowed *Mini Finger* patio carrots in early August, which cropped from late October until after Christmas as there was nothing more than light frost. The largest carrots were, as their name suggests, the size of little fingers and of excellent flavour – delicious in winter salad. Carrots are a useful crop in terms of rotation, to give containers a rest from growing leaves (see Chapter 2, pages 26-27).

Another option, of which there are many in early August, would have been to sow or plant rocket, winter purslane, spinach or endive and oriental leaves such as mizuna, pak choi and mustard.

Leaf lettuce and chicories in a window box

In a plastic window box measuring 48x23cm (19x9"), I planted one each of *Grenoble Red, Freckles, Bergamo* and *Bijou* in early April. They cropped from late April until late July – about 10 medium-sized leaves per week on average. The plants were kept small by frequent harvesting: which helped reduce the need to water.

Spring radish grows fast and you can eat the leaves, though hairy!

I uprooted the flowering stems and then pretended to be on holiday until 22 August, when I replanted the window box with three leaf chicories and an endive, harvesting a few small leaves in early September, then about eight to ten weekly through October and half that through the winter.

Basil and rocket in terracotta window boxes

In a terracotta window box measuring 31x16cm (12x6"), I set out two red basil plants in late June, and enjoyed small pickings through the summer, which was a cool season and not beneficial to basil. Last pickings were in early October. In another similar box, I planted two *Skyrocket* on 22 August and it took only 10 days for them to produce a few small leaves. Harvests were steady through September, a little smaller in October and occasional thereafter. I didn't line the terracotta with plastic, so needed to water regularly, even in midwinter.

Mixed salad leaves in a window box

On 20 June in a PVC window box measuring 210x110cm (7'x3'6"), I planted one each of red basil, *Nufari* green basil, curly parsley, three lettuces – *Grenoble Red, Freckles* and *Mottistone* – and two endives, *Bianca Riccia da Taglio* and *Fine de Louviers*. Leaves were gathered from early July,

Six weeks of harvests already by late spring. The marbled lettuce is *Mottistone*.

occasionally quite large handfuls. The lettuce was starting to flower by late August so I removed it and planted baby leaf kohlrabi, *Fairway* rocket and sowed red-stemmed leaf radish on 27 August.

By about 8 September it was apparent that the large parsley and endive plants were rooting more powerfully than the young salads and depriving them of nutrients, so although they were still cropping well, I twisted them out and planted mizuna, *Apollo* rocket, red-stemmed leaf radish and tatsoi instead, to have all young plants of the same size growing together. First leaves picked on 18 October weighed about 80g (3 oz); thereafter pickings were somewhat less, although consistent – enough for garnish more than a meal.

Beetroot, then leaf lettuce in a terracotta pot

In a 36cm (14") diameter pot I planted module-raised *Boltardy* beetroot in late April, yielding 620g (1lb 6oz) of sweet, baby roots by early July. On 14 July I planted four lettuces – *Grenoble Red, Maravilla de Verano, Nymans* and *Roselee* – of which the last was eaten by slugs, and I subsequently picked leaves weekly until early November. The highest harvest was 170g (6 oz) on 29 August.

BABY LEAVES (ALSO CALLED MICRO LEAVES AND LIVING LEAVES)

For the quickest results and in the smallest of spaces, you can grow seedling salad, either by cutting whole baby plants or by harvesting their tiny leaves. Less compost is needed to grow them, and sowing to harvest is less than three weeks for brassicas in summer. Two seed trays on the window sill, alternately sown and harvested, could keep you in a sprinkling of saladings from late April until November.

Greenhouse micro-leaf bed 1.2x1.05m (4'x3'6")

To explore the possibilities of different leaves, I created a bed in the greenhouse on top of a pallet, just over a metre square and lined with old fleece. Sides were made by screwing some old 15cm (6") planks to the pallet's edges. After gently firming the 6cm (2") of multipurpose compost, I marked 15cm intervals along all the sides and then ran a small bamboo between them, across the top of the compost, to mark out a grid pattern of 56 15cm squares.

First sowing

On 6 August I sowed different seeds in each square, except for twelve that were sown three days later when more seeds arrived in the post. It is hard to sow precisely and a few squares had over fifty seeds in. A week later I realized that some seed was too thickly sown, so I thinned out baby seedlings to a spacing

of about one plant every 2cm (1") – about thirty plants per 15cm square.

Just over two weeks later, in thinning out the too-thick sowings, I harvested a bowl of wonderfully varied baby seedlings, comprising a huge range of tastes, by cutting them just above the compost with an extremely sharp knife. Careful cutting avoids any uprooting and may avoid the need to wash leaves, while a layer of vermiculite on top of the compost is an optional extra to help the harvest stay clean.

By 25 August the bed was groaning with leaves, especially its 24 members of the fast-growing cabbage family. I harvested 600g (1lb 5oz) and should have picked more, but our appetites could not keep up with the new growth. On 3 September I cut 1.2kg (2lb 10oz) of rather larger leaves for the local pub, then another 700g (1lb 8oz) of regrowth a week later. By this stage many plants had been cut close to or below their growing point of smallest leaves, meaning that harvests were becoming smaller and harder to gather among the increasing number of older, yellowing leaves. So I pulled out all stems and roots, shaking off any loose compost before starting again.

Second sowing

After spreading another 1cm (½") of compost, I resowed from late September for autumn leaves. There were four leaves on most plants by 29 October, when I picked and cut a small bucketful of baby leaves, 550g (1lb 3oz) in weight, from the faster-growing plants such as leaf radish, mustard, rocket, mizuna and mibuna.

Small pickings were then taken every

Salads for micro or baby leaves, 11 days after sowing in the greenhouse in August.

Just five days later, leaves are now mostly baby size.

week in November, between 110 and 150g of baby leaves, mostly cut. Growth thereafter was slower but plants stayed healthy and offered occasional small harvests. You can either cut across the top where close growth has resulted in many tiny leaves – often the case with mustards and mizuna – or pick leaf by leaf where they are larger, often possible with leaf radish and *Apollo* rocket.

By mid-December some lower leaves were yellow and the bed was running low in nutrients. Had I wanted to continue, it would have been worth spreading the old compost on beds in the garden and starting afresh with new compost.

Tips on growing baby leaves

* For continuous supply, EITHER sow little and often – say, every two to three weeks – and cut young plants at stem level, OR grow in a larger, slightly deeper bed or container and harvest carefully (above the growing point).
* Cutting baby plants at stem level means immediate resowing, whereas allowing them to grow a little more and picking or cutting some of their baby leaves allows another small harvest or two.
* Stems of baby plants have juicy sap of appealing flavour.
* Some unusual flavours include carrot tops, red cabbage, lovage, radish, fennel and Mesembryanthemum (aka Livingstone daisy). Any plant listed in Chapter 5 can be used.
* Flavours of baby leaves are true to type, subtly different and milder than flavours of larger leaves.

Special tips for seedlings in seed trays

Every winter I record leaf harvests from seed trays and old mushroom boxes in the greenhouse. A seed tray of kales, chicory, endive and sorrel yielded 220g (8 oz) of leaves in five small harvests between December and April. The mushroom trays, growing plants such as mizuna, mibuna, rocket and leaf radish, produce 500-600g (18–21oz) each over the same period.

* Seed trays work well in small areas for growing selections of baby leaves. Fill them to about three-quarters depth with multipurpose compost. Two or three harvests is a reasonable target.
* Cress and brassicas (mizuna, rocket, mustards, cabbages, kales, etc.), are the quickest, as well as the easiest to harvest.
* Thickly sown carpets of seedlings need cutting before the first true leaves are fully grown; otherwise there may be a lot of yellowing cotyledons in the harvest. Sow more thinly if you want plants to grow their true leaves.
* Red amaranth is an excellent plant for some vivid colour in summer and autumn.
* Old mushroom boxes, which are deeper than seed trays, can be lined with cardboard or polythene, filled with compost and sown more thinly – say, one plant every 2.5cm (1") – for repeated picking of small leaves. Or set just six plants in each box and pick outer leaves regularly.

CHAPTER FIVE

LEAF FLAVOURS

AN AMAZING PALETTE TO CHOOSE FROM

Brief summary

* Certain groups of leaves share many taste characteristics.
* The large cabbage family is characterized by a spicy, mustard flavour, more pronounced as leaves grow larger and older.
* Chicories and endives possess a range of flavours but are all more or less bitter, especially as leaves rather than hearts.
* Plants of spinach and beets have strongly flavoured and rather metallic-tasting leaves.
* Many herbs are mild enough to enjoy with salad leaves, and there is a huge range of flavours.
* There is a most interesting group of other leaves that boast some appealing tastes, such as pea shoots, purslane and corn salad (lamb's lettuce).

The tasting notes below will, I hope, point you towards those leaves you most enjoy – there are certainly plenty to choose from.

The table overleaf gives an overall picture of the depth and quality of flavour of different leaves. Pungency is from left to right, while leaves with strength of flavour, and sometimes bitterness and acidity, are towards the bottom.

For example, *Green in the Snow* mustard is the hottest leaf here and sorrel is the most acid, while lamb's lettuce is the mildest, in my opinion!

Red Giant mustard, kept small by frequent picking!

LEAF FLAVOURS		
Mild flavour (mildest at top)	**Some heat**	**Hot mustard**
Lamb's lettuce (corn salad), Chinese cabbage		
Lettuce	Leaf radish	Rocket
Purslane	Pak choi	*Ruby Streaks*
Pea shoots, mizuna, *Red Russian* kale		*Golden Streaks*
Mitsuba, spinach, chards, tatsoi	Komatsuna, mibuna	*Red Giant*
Endives, chicories		*Green in the Snow*
Parsley		Cress
Chervil		Coriander
Basil	Dill	
Sorrel		

DESCRIPTIONS OF LEAVES FROM 3-4-WEEK-OLD PLANTS

Brassicas (cabbage family)

Chinese broccoli *Kailaan*
Tall-growing, mild and juicy with a slight mustard flavour.

Chinese cabbage *Kiansi, Kaboko F1*
Large, rounded leaves, thick and slightly hairy with a succulent, mild, watery flavour. By a month old it also has crunchy, tasty white stems.

Kale *Nero di Toscana* (also called *Black Cabbage* or *Cavolo Nero*)
Dark and thin, spicy and pungent. A good chew.

Kale *Red Russian*
Mild flavour and, unlike most other kales, leaves are tender and smooth, with pretty mauve and feathery leaves.

Kohlrabi, purple varieties
Leaves actually taste of kohlrabi, rooty and turnip-like in a pleasing way.

Komatsuna (Japanese mustard spinach)
Long-stemmed and oval-shaped, of cabbage flavour but mild and watery when young. A slight crunch.

Mibuna
Thin-leaved and tender, becoming pungent as the leaves rapidly grow larger.

Mizuna *Kyoto*
Feathery leaves are tender, mild, soft and watery with long white stems.

Mizuna *Namenia*
Juicy and watery, slightly mustard-like, with quite large leaves.

Mizuna *Sessantina*
A larger-leaved and similar-tasting mizuna, crunchy-stemmed and mild with just a hint of cabbage in young leaves.

August planting of *Pizzo* mustard, red and green pak choi, *Red Frills* mustard.

Mustard *Golden Streaks / Green Frills*
Bright green and feathery, juicy and mild initially but with a hot aftertaste.

Mustard *Green in the Snow*
Hot and spicy as a small leaf, becoming extremely pungent as plants mature. An aftertaste of horseradish.

Mustard *Red Giant*
Hot, even when small-leaved. More green than red in warm weather.

Mustard *Ruby Streaks / Red Frills / Red Lace*
Agreeable and bittersweet, followed by a hot aftertaste. Darker and more ruby in cold weather.

Pak choi *Joi Coi F1, Hanakan*
Mild and crunchy, especially its thick white stem.

Radish *French Breakfast*
Small hairs and a mild radish flavour.

Radish leaf *Sai Sai*
Smoother and larger than *French Breakfast*, pleasantly mild, a hint of radish to taste and a faintly hot aftertaste.

Rape, salad
Tender and tastes like mizuna. Agreeable flavour and fast-growing.

Red cabbage, leaves of seedlings
More tender, sweeter and milder than larger cabbage leaves.

Rocket, salad
Mild as a baby leaf, quickly heating up as it grows, often a little sweet.

Rocket, wild
More pungent than salad rocket with thinner leaves and a later harvest.

Tatsoi *Tah Sai*
Compact, crunchy plants. Pretty, mild and watery with a slight aromatic flavour.

Tatsoi *Yukina Savoy*
Larger, mild-flavoured leaves, chewier than *Tah Sai* with a tannic aftertaste.

March outside, hardy winter purslane and land cress, netted against pests.

Young salad rocket in a window box, sown August.

Texel greens
Mild and sweet, with a similar size and appearance to rape – oval-shaped, slightly waxy, mid-green leaves.
Turnip
The young leaves are mild and tender, with gentle turnip flavour.

Spinach / chard / beet

Beetroot *Boltardy* and *Vulkan Red Beet*
A strong taste of beetroot, pungent. A few leaves go a long way.
Chard *Rainbow*
Lightly tannic and acid, of metallic flavour. Best eaten with other leaves.
Spinach *Campania* and *Medania*
Tender leaves and juicy, sweet in cold weather, flavours of iron and tannin, piquant aftertaste.

Chicories, endives

Chicory *Catalogna*
Thin and tender, more bitter than sweet, balanced by slight acidity.
Chicory *Da Taglio Bionda*
Thin, smooth leaves are markedly bitter and best used in small amounts.
Chicory *Treviso Svelta*
Prettily speckled, bittersweet and tender, long and thick-stemmed.
Chicory *Zuccherina di Trieste*
Not as sweet as its name suggests!
Dandelion *Red-ribbed*
Long and thin, rather acid and bitter but full of flavour.
Endive *Bianca Riccia da Taglio*
Pale yellow, tender and mildly bittersweet.
Endive *Romanesco*
A fuller flavour than the chicories;

slightly less bitter with long, serrated leaves.

Herbs

Burnet, salad
Small, slightly bitter and tannic.
Chervil, plain-leaved
Mild and fresh with a taste of aniseed that lingers agreeably.
Coriander *Cruiser*
Large, tender leaves, juicy texture and mild flavour.
Dill *Dukat*
Compact, feathery leaves and a mild, minty flavour; different from mature leaves, which pack more punch and have a sharp bite.
Fennel, common
When small and tender the leaves offer a full fennel flavour, slightly more pungent as it matures.
Lovage, no named variety
Bittersweet and many layers of flavour, with a great range of aromatic tastes. Impressive.
Parsley, moss curled
A slightly stronger, more pungent flavour than plain- or flat-leaved, with a sweet aftertaste.
Parsley, plain-leaved
Mild and slightly acid with aromatic hints of fragrant drying grass.
Sorrel *Broad-leaved*
Rich lemon flavours, slightly acid and mouth-tingling.
Sorrel *Buckler-leaved*
Small, tender leaves that have a fantastic mouth-filling taste of lemon, with a juicy acidity.

Baby leaves of root vegetables

Beetroot – see page 55.
Carrot *Early Nantes*
Lovely hint of sweetness to a quite deep flavour of carrot, slightly acid.
Fennel, bulb *Montebianco*
Feathery leaves with intriguing minty, aniseed flavours.
Parsnip *White Gem*
Pungent baby leaves with an unmistakable flavour of parsnip and a rather bitter aftertaste.

Other

Amaranth *Garnet Red*
Handsome tiny and dark red leaves with some variegations. Chewy with a grassy flavour, rather dull and flat.
Cress *Cressida*
Tall and spindly with a hot, spicy taste and lingering aromas.
Lamb's lettuce (corn salad) *D'Orlanda*
Mild, firm-textured and slightly waxy.
Lettuce *Grenoble Red*
Gentle aromatic flavour, slightly bitter and tannic, no powerful aftertastes. Most lettuces have consistently mild flavours, with only small varietal difference. Batavians such as *Maravilla de Verano (Canasta)* and *Grenoble Red* are perhaps the most interesting. Hearted lettuces such as *Little Gem* and *Lobjoits* have sweetness as well.
Mesembryanthemum *Magic Carpet*
Pretty reddish stems, so soft they almost melt in the mouth; watery and fresh with a hint of acidity.
Mitsuba (Japanese parsley)
Herby with hints of parsley, celery and

We planted tiny seedlings of salad rocket among the still-cropping lettuce.

Lettuce *Grenoble Red* forming a heart of sweeter leaves.

other herbs combining in a subtle way.

Pea *Ambassador*

Short and dark green shoots, juicy and with rich pea flavour.

Pea *Tall Sugar*

Longer and paler shoots, a little sweeter, tender and succulent. The pea flavours are really delicious.

Purslane *Green*

Pretty and juicy with a crunchy stem and pleasant citric tang that explodes in a mild way as one bites into it.

Tree spinach *Chenopodium*

Very mild. Tastes more like Mesembryanthemum than spinach.

GLOSSARY OF TERMS

Acid equates to tangy, sharp, clean and sour. These slightly derogatory terms are misleading because small doses of clean acidity are refreshing and contribute to the balance of other tastes when used in the right proportion.

Aftertaste is the sensation of flavour that lingers when food has been swallowed, and it may reveal different flavours from those experienced when food is still in the mouth.

Citric is a description of certain acid tastes, which are most commonly found in lemons and limes.

Pungent, mustardy tastes can be aggressively dominant and need respect. They often surface as hot aftertastes behind other, milder flavours that have expressed themselves, and they may linger in the mouth for a time.

Sour – see *acid* above.

Sweet tastes are rare but welcome in salad leaves, especially when they balance the bitterness of chicories and endives. They are most common in hearts and can be augmented by blanching any leaves, excluding all light for a week or so.

FLAVOUR CHANGES WITH MATURITY

The mildest flavours are found in young, small leaves, and even the cotyledons of certain herbs, such as lovage, are packed full of taste and aroma.

The development of flavour as leaves grow and plants mature is to be welcomed if you like stronger flavours, and is especially pronounced in the cabbage family. Baby rocket leaves are utterly different from large ones, and also from small leaves of older rocket plants, which can be surprisingly hot. If you want mild flavours of certain fast-growing brassica salads, you need to pick them frequently to keep leaves small, especially in warm weather, and to resow at intervals.

The other way in which maturity affects flavour is the sweetening of leaves in hearting plants. Sweetness is the least common element of taste found in salad leaves, but the pale hearts of lettuce, endive and chicory have enough sugars to create a wonderful balance and depth of flavour

FLAVOUR CHANGES WITH SEASON

It is intriguing that each season clearly defines the flavours of salad leaves, when plants are grown at their best time. There are two elements to this:

* Firstly, the flavours of some leaves change with the seasons. Cold weather, for instance, has a sweetening effect on many endives and chicories. In frosty weather some plants produce sugars as antifreeze, and spinach leaves become almost sugary. In addition it can happen that we perceive flavours differently as our bodies adapt to changing weather and day length.

* Secondly, the leaves of each season have their own overall characteristic flavour. Spring shows the greatest rhythm of change as strong tasting winter leaves make way for more subtle and fragrant new ones. The dominance of lettuce in late spring and summer makes for a thirst-quenching quality to salad leaves of less flavour, punctuated by exciting aromas of herbs and other plants. Autumn brings stronger flavours again as brassicas, chicories and endives arrive in season. Both pungency and bitterness are freely available in cool weather and they become stronger in winter as leaf size and wateriness are reduced. I do wonder if the powerful flavours of winter leaves are a reflection of their ability to help our bodies withstand periods of cold and darkness. The arrival of fragrant new growth in spring brings new sparkle and vitality.

Take a look at Part Two for information on the best times to sow all these different leaves and a fuller idea of how to create your favourite seasonal salads.

CHAPTER SIX

SOWING, RAISING, SUSTAINING

HEALTHY PLANTS, INDOORS AND OUTDOORS

Brief summary

* Outdoor sowing is more weather-dependent than indoor sowing.
* Seed of different salads in each season can be sown outdoors from about mid-March to mid-September.
* Indoor sowings can be done in different sorts of covered spaces, preferably with full daylight.
* There is a variety of growing media, compost and sowing techniques.
* Growing in modules gives reliable plants that transplant easily.
* Diseases of small plants are rare, but slugs need careful surveillance.

Early growth from seed is tender and often slow, so a plant's first tiny leaves are vulnerable to grazing by slugs and, since they are so small, it takes just one nibble for the whole plant to disappear. Such disappearances are often blamed on poor germination but close examination may reveal a few thin, pale stalks.

Because of this, it is often more reliable to raise plants in a protected environment before setting them out in beds or pots. Plus, more cropping time is gained by not having to wait for plants to grow *in situ* from seed. This is explained in detail on pages 65-71.

New seedlings in June: mostly lettuce, all pricked out from trays.

SOWING OUTDOORS

If you have no indoor facilities, look carefully at this section for guidelines on which outdoor sowings work best and in which season. For example, spinach and chard in the spring and oriental leaves in late summer often work well from direct sowing.

The timing of your first outdoor sowings is never written in stone because it depends on many variable factors:

* Weather varies from spring to spring and can postpone first sowings by two or three weeks. March is the month when one starts looking for opportunities, but stormy conditions with lashings of cold rain, or regular frost at night, invite a wait for better weather. On average in most of Britain I recommend first sowings between 10 March and 10 April, depending also on your plot.

* Soil conditions play a major role. If your allotment or garden has a poorly drained clay soil which lies wet, it will take longer to warm up and enable seedlings to grow than, for example, the test beds and containers featured in Chapters 3 and 4. Their soft, friable compost allows free passage of any heavy rain, and the dark colour of compost is quicker than a light-coloured soil to heat up in any sun. This makes growth earlier, stronger and more likely to survive pests.

* The situation of growing media must also be considered. If containers or your garden are mostly shaded from the spring sun, I recommend sowing a week or two later.

The first outdoor planting of lettuce in early spring, subsequently fleeced over.

BEST OUTDOOR SOWING DATES						
March (from mid-month)	April	May	June	July	August	September (all before mid-month)
Lettuce	Lettuce	Lettuce	Lettuce	Lettuce	Lettuce (after mid-month for overwintering only)	Mizuna and some other oriental leaves
Spinach	Spinach	Spinach	Chards	Spinach	Spinach (until mid-month)	Rocket
Chards	Chards	Chards	Certain varieties of endives, leaf and heart	Chards	Chards (until mid-month)	Lamb's lettuce (corn salad)
Peas, for shoots	Peas	Orache	Leaf chicory	Any endive	All endives (until about the 10th)	Winter purslane
Orache	Orache	Certain varieties of endives	Certain varieties of radicchio	Any radicchio	Leaf endive (until about the 20th)	Land cress
Parsley	Parsley	Leaf chicory	Chicory (for forcing next winter)	Sugarloaf chicory	Kale	
Coriander	Coriander	Chicory (for forcing next winter)	Kale	Kale	Rocket	
Dill	Dill	Parsley	Parsley	Chinese cabbage	Oriental leaves	
Sorrel	Sorrel	Dill	Dill	Rocket (better at month's end)	Lamb's lettuce	
		Sorrel	Sorrel	Oriental leaves (better at month's end)	Turnip, for leaves	
			Basil	Lamb's lettuce (better at month's end)	Parsley (early in the month)	
			Amaranth	Purslane	Sorrel (early in the month)	
			Purslane	Parsley	Chervil (early in the month)	
				Dill	Winter purslane	
				Sorrel	Land cress	
				Chervil (better at month's end)		

These observations relate to dates of sowings in spring and late autumn only. Sowing dates in summer and early autumn are mostly governed by day length, as opposed to weather, and do not vary from year to year.

A wonderful thing is that spring sowings can 'catch up'. A mid-March sowing of spinach that suffers cold winds and rain may crop only a little before an early-April sowing that enjoyed steady warmth. The variability of weather brings an element of uncertainty to all early and late sowing dates. If you are interested in considering the effects of the moon when working out your sowing dates, have a look at Chapter 7.

FIRST OUTDOOR SOWINGS IN SPRING

These are mainly of spinach, chards, peas and lettuce, and also perhaps one sowing of rapid-growing mizuna, which just has time to crop before the longer days make it rise to flower, and before flea beetles become too numerous. Early spinach sowings are best, with varieties such as *Tarpy, Medania* (round leaves) and *Galaxy* (pointed leaves), whose growth is especially fast. They need frequent picking if you want to keep eating small leaves and will crop for about a month before flowering, so make a second sowing four to six weeks after the first one.

Lettuce is much longer-lasting if you pick its leaves carefully. I thin seedlings to about 20cm apart in rows 25cm apart (8x10"), which allows me to pick off outer leaves for up to three months before flowering. A second sowing of lettuce can therefore wait until about 10 weeks after the first one, often in late May.

On the other hand, if you don't thin lettuce and cut across the rows of close-growing seedlings, they develop more mildew on the bottom leaves and run out of room to grow, making them flower somewhat earlier. Hence more sowings are necessary and the second one needs to be about six weeks after the first. For lettuce hearts, three-week intervals are necessary on average, but only ten days in July.

LATER OUTDOOR SOWINGS

A basic calendar of outdoor sowing is set out on the preceding page. The trickiest month is August because the frequency of sowing increases as day length diminishes rapidly, so that missing a week in August will delay cropping in autumn by up to three weeks. Missing a week in September is even more dramatic. If you want salad in the winter half of the year, it is important to be on the ball through late summer and early autumn.

Although lettuce, endives, chicories and spinach can still be sown until about mid-August, many sowings at summer's end are of the cabbage family – rocket, oriental leaves and kales – which thrive in the relative absence of flea beetles and then in damper autumn weather with shorter days.

Slow-growing lamb's lettuce (corn salad) is a staple throughout winter and can be sown until about mid-Septem-

The potted-on stage in mid-May and just before planting out: basil, cucumber, pepper, squash.

ber. Two other possibilities are land cress for small amounts of leaves with strong flavour, and winter purslane, for unusual texture. Coriander and chervil are good winter herbs that have a long life before flowering if sown in mid-August – but their production of winter leaves will be small unless given some shelter from the weather (see Chapter 17, pages 211-12).

Final outdoor sowings are sometime in the middle of September, when rocket and mizuna are probably the most likely to succeed and to continue growing slowly through any mild winter weather. Later sowings can give small harvests but depend on the autumn being warm. Within these timelines, we can find even better sowing dates thanks to the moon (see Chapter 7).

SOWING INDOORS

The advantages

Using covered spaces for sowing is rather more work, but brings many benefits:

* Faster and more reliable germination enables earlier cropping in spring, when leaves are often at a premium.
* Raising plants in a separate growing space enables rapid successional cropping, because you can have plants ready to set out as soon as an earlier batch of plants has reached the end of its life. This avoids periods of scarcity while waiting for seedlings to establish.
* Slugs can be avoided; it is easier to keep most plant-raising spaces clean than the whole garden.

Potting three-week-old basil to larger modules.

The same basil, 12 days later, with organic seed on the right.

* Pests in general are less problematic than with outdoor sowings, because seedlings that grow strongly in ideal conditions are of less interest to predators.

Suitable spaces

Locations for indoor sowing are varied and their use is more fully explained in Chapter 19, pages 232-33. They are listed here briefly in order of effectiveness and ease of use:

* Glass greenhouses are lovely to work in, have excellent light levels, and hold on to a little more heat at night than most plastic-coated structures.
* Polytunnels warm up well by day but lose heat rapidly at sunset. Their light levels are mostly good if the polythene is wiped annually.
* Conservatories usually have light on one side only, so growth may be less solid, but they are often warmer than outdoor structures. If it is a smart conservatory, remember that raising plants can be a slightly messy and watery business!
* Cold frames and cloches are effective at helping earlier growth but are more difficult to manage – slugs often invade and there is no room for the gardener to work in them under cover.
* Window sills are warm and cosy but can be somewhat lacking in daylight, making for leggy growth with long, fragile stems, so plants must be moved to full light before they are too big. As with conservatories, watering can create mess.

Materials needed

* Seed trays have holes in the bottom to allow excess moisture to drain out; too much water is inimical to seedlings, which may then 'damp off', the term used for the often fatal attacks of mildew on baby leaves. It is best to water seed trays at the start of a bright day when sunlight will soon evaporate water from the surface of small leaves. Seedlings can be 'pricked out' into modules or pots when they have just two leaves and no more than 2-3 cm (an inch or so) of root. Gently squash the root into a pencil-sized hole in compost-filled modules, holding the seedling by its leaf, never by its tender stem.
* Module or plug trays enable the roots of each plant to grow independently, allowing rapid, undisturbed and more pest-free growth after planting. They come in various shapes and sizes – any number between 24 and 60 partitions in an A4-sized tray is good for small but sturdy plants. When filling them, press compost in firmly so that a compact and extensive root system can develop. Drainage is good in modules and damping off should be rare. Like seed trays they are usually made of plastic or polystyrene, which can be used time and again if handled gently, without any washing or cleaning. Small plugs or pots made of coir or other natural materials can be planted in their entirety but are more expensive as they serve only once.
* I recommend organic, multipurpose potting compost if you can find it,

because I believe that natural sources of nutrients are better balanced, and because their basic media are mostly recycled waste products. This may result in some weed growth, and the same is often true of sieved home-made compost. Special composts for sowing often include sharp sand or other ingredients to increase drainage.

* A good watering can is vital and a good rose is essential, because it is important to distribute water evenly and gently, with good control so that over- and under-watering are avoided. Watering is a skill to learn and you need to develop an awareness of the needs of your plants by watching the weather above all: plants may require as much water in two sunny days as in a dull week.

* Extra heat is required only in late winter and early spring, and it is not vital. Conservatories and window sills have enough ambient heat, so they can be good to germinate seedlings and get them underway – the first two weeks is when heat is most useful to aid in germination and establishment.

* Tool-wise I recommend a pencil for any pricking out and then a dibber for making holes to set plants into ground, bed or container.

ON USING MODULES

Modules or plugs are a fantastic way of raising plants. Each one can develop healthy leaves and a strong root system, which survives intact when planted out.

This helps to sustain it after planting, in the face of cold nights, dry days and attack by slugs. Plants can be set out at their final spacing with no need for later thinning, and where weeds are a problem you will gain a significant head start. Plants can be raised earlier, their growth is more predictable and less seed is used because germination is usually more even and successful.

It is highly worthwhile to spend time and money on raising good plants because they are at least half of the story of successful harvests.

PLANTING OUT

Use a dibber or small trowel to make a hole in the soil slightly larger and deeper than the root system of the plant and its compost, then push it in firmly with stem, using the spacings given in Part Three. Water in gently unless it is about to rain. See also the advice at the end of this chapter.

After planting them out and before picking begins there is a period called 'growing on', which is often remarkably brief for salad plants.

GROWING ON

If you have sown your seed or grown your plants in their right season, they pass quickly from being tender youngsters to a stage of early maturity when the first leaves can be harvested. Salads are almost the only vegetable to make the transition so speedily – there is relatively little waiting involved, unless you want large leaves.

SLUGS

The main pest is often slugs and picking them off by torchlight is an effective way of reducing their population – on three or four successive nights if possible. On the first night you may be surprised at their numbers and level of activity. See Chapter 8, pages 76-84 for more details.

ANTS

Ants are less rapid than slugs in their depredations, but harder to control, partly because of their sheer weight of numbers. Again, see Chapter 8, page 84.

WEEDING

Two ongoing jobs are weeding and watering, both dependent on the weather. Damp weather encourages weeds to germinate and also makes hoeing ineffective, but large quantities of salad leaves grow in such small areas that weeds should rarely be a major problem. Simply pull out any you see while picking leaves. Remove them small so that they do not shelter slugs, or compete with salad plants for moisture and nutrients.

WATERING

As long as your soil is well composted, watering is only necessary in prolonged dry weather or extreme heat. At these times, a good soak every few days is as viable as a daily sprinkle and is a more efficient use of water, because surface evaporation happens less regularly.

Should it become truly hot and sunny – say, 25°C (77°F) or higher – watering

Lettuce seedlings early March. They were sown three weeks ago and pricked out into these modules a week ago.

Basil direct sown in modules above, and to prick out from a seed tray below.

every two days is worthwhile and containers will probably require water every day, as their limited volume of compost can hold less water than beds and garden soil.

It is an interesting paradox that although salad leaves are mostly water, they often grow better in fine weather because extra sunlight encourages stronger, healthier growth; whereas in wet weather there is often too high a proportion of water to light, making leaves more sappy and less resistant to pests. We can add water in dry weather but we cannot add sunlight in wet weather!

FIRST HARVESTS

How to decide when your salad plants are ready to tolerate removal of a leaf or two? They need to have grown to the point where there are sufficient roots to rapidly enlarge existing small leaves and to make new ones. For well-spaced lettuce, this means a plant the size of a side plate with about ten leaves altogether, of which up to four can be removed at one pick. Plant size is important as well as leaf number – rocket and spinach have fewer and larger leaves, mizuna has more, smaller ones.

If you have sown thick rows and plan to cut across the top of them, to give you a harvest of small, tender leaves, start cutting before or as soon as you see some yellowing of leaves at the bottom. This should give plenty of small leaves, and another two or three cuts, providing the knife or scissors always pass just above the top of plants' tiniest leaves.

A rule of thumb is that leaves should be picked when they start touching the leaves of neighbouring plants, for three reasons:

* They are large enough.
* Slug numbers will be prevented from increasing when soil or compost becomes covered over by leaves.
* Lower leaves that are deprived of light will begin to yellow and suffer fungal problems.

See Chapter 2, pages 22-3 for more detailed information on ways of gathering salad leaves.

FINAL FLOWERING

Picking leaves off the same plant can continue for weeks and months, until central stems begin to elongate and rise upwards, indicating that plants are finally ready to flower and set seed.

When you follow my guidelines for sowing plants in their right seasons, and for regularly picking their leaves, this flowering can be delayed sufficiently to give you the most worthwhile harvest of leaves. They should be of a superb freshness and quality, with minimal damage from pests – see also Chapters 7 and 8 for more details on boosting the health of your plants, and on coping with pests.

INDOOR SOWING DATES FOR EARLIER SALAD OUTDOORS

If you wish, all the salads in the table on page 63 can also be sown indoors, while the ones listed below require extra warmth when sown in the months listed here. In an outdoor greenhouse or polytunnel, these dates work best with the provision of a little extra heat (see also Chapter 18).

JANUARY	FEBRUARY	MID-APRIL	MAY
Lettuce	Lettuce	Basil	Basil
Spinach	Spinach		Amaranth
Mizuna	Mizuna		Purslane
Parsley	Orache		
	Parsley		
	Peas		

PLANTING INDOOR-SOWN PLANTS

Indoor-grown plants may come ready to plant out when conditions outdoors are cold and windy. But fear not, because fleece/row cover makes all the difference when planting in such conditions, protecting them from lashing winds and extremes of cold. There is no need to prewarm beds or to harden off plants. Simply set them in cold soil and lay fleece on top, held in place by stones or posts or clips, for up to a month after planting.

Plants are happier when fleece is held firmly on top of them than when it is loosely flapping in the wind or held up by hoops. Just make sure to plant into clean soil and compost, with no hiding-places for slugs, which are happy under fleece and also love tender, newly arrived plants. Keep a careful eye out for them during your salads' first two weeks outside (see Chapter 8).

CHAPTER SEVEN

COSMIC LEAVES

BRINGING NEW ENERGY TO SOIL, PLANTS AND OURSELVES

THE MOON

Moon forces are as mysterious to Western civilizations as is the power of water. Both are intimately related, as tidal movements remind us all the time. Salad leaves are mostly water, so the moon's behaviour is worth paying attention to.

I have grappled with understanding the best way to work with the phases of the moon. They are constantly transmitting different energies, starting with the most obvious dichotomy of waxing and waning.

Waxing/waning

Waxing moons are associated with qualities of expansion, vigour and masculinity. Waning moons are associated with qualities of contraction, passivity and femininity.

Big, bold salad leaves should therefore come from sowings made in the fortnight or so of a waxing moon (see the following pages). Those sown during a waning moon should have smaller leaves and perhaps more extensive roots. This understanding creates an approximately fortnightly rhythm and changeover points, with the whole cycle from new moon to new moon taking 29.5 days.

Summer evening at Homeacres, almost a full moon.

The zodiac

Many gardeners sow by different moon phases, created as it crosses the field of heavenly constellations that we see from Earth. During the two or three days in front of each one, the moon picks up and transmits one of their four different qualities: earth, air, water and fire. These translate into encouraging one main aspect of plants' growth: roots, flowers, leaves or fruits/seeds respectively.

For salad leaves we should look to sow seeds when the moon is in front of one of the three water constellations – Pisces, Cancer and Scorpio. This way of understanding moon forces involves a more rapid rhythm and 'leaf days' reoccur about every 10 days.

Ascending/descending

A third change in the moon's behaviour is its height in the sky, which varies from high to low and back again every 27.3 days, just as the sun varies over 365 days. When living in France I noticed that many old Gascon farmers paid more attention to this than to waxing and waning. In particular, planting out and moving plants is better during a descending moon because root development is favoured during that fortnight.

Other periodicities

Further moon happenings serve to complicate the picture even more, such as apogee and perigee as the moon moves closer to and further away from Earth. Its conjunctions with and oppositions to other planets, especially Saturn, also bring different qualities into play, as does the hour of moonrise. Discover more with a biodynamic planting calendar or wall-chart (see Resources).

MOON RESEARCH

Many farmers, gardeners and scientists have run experiments where seeds are sown at different times, principally according to waxing/waning and to the zodiac, but also to the time of moonrise. Astronomer Nick Kollerstrom describes these succinctly (see Resources) and they give plenty of food for thought.

Over 70 years ago there was a stunning piece of work conducted by a Russian scientist called Lilly Kolisko, first published in 1936 (see Resources). Ms Kolisko worked closely with the Anthroposophical Agricultural Foundation in Stuttgart and grew many different plants over a decade, sowing them at all different phases of the moon. Interestingly, she was principally looking at waxing and waning, asking herself this simple question:

"The forces which stream through the earth at full moon must differ from those at new moon. Does the plant respond in its growth to these forces or does it not?"

Kolisko's results

One major conclusion stood out above all others: growth of plants that were sown **two days before full moon** resulted in the greatest encapsulation and expression of moon forces. Plants

Unfolding a heart of *Palla Rossa* chicory.

Her book is full of photographs of many different farm and garden plants sown at different moon phases, at different stages of growth, repeated year after year in both laboratory and open ground, and all demonstrating the same result.

Implications

This carefully conducted, extensive and well-documented research has a clear message: growth is strongest from sowing two days before full moon. But what if you are on holiday or otherwise occupied at that moment? How can a grower like me sow everything in one day? Or if the soil is dry, moon forces cannot enter! There is much food for thought here.

In broad terms, I aim to sow and set out salad plants in the waxing fortnight, two days before full moon when possible, as well as paying attention to the qualities associated with each constellation.

And most of all, I like to work with my green fingers, fertilizing the garden with gratitude, goodwill and continual amazement at abundant, healthy growth. Gardening at Homeacres is a combination of the weather, my thoughts, my actions, the water I use and the moon timings I cooperate with. This is about cultivating health, as much as avoiding pest and disease.

See Resources for pointers on finding out more about the moon and water.

sown then were larger and more productive of leaves, flowers, fruits and roots. Notable differences in vigour lasted to the end of their lives and were such that, for example, maize sown two days before new moon matured later and grew smaller than maize sown a fortnight or fifteen days later, but two days before full moon.

Two days before full and new moons is the high point of waxing and waning forces respectively, but translates to seeds only if the soil is and remains damp at that time. Water is needed to carry moon forces into Earth.

Sowing on the actual day of full moon acquaints seeds with a moon that is just beginning to ebb. Kolisko found the waning influence to build up until two days before new moon, when its peak lasted a day at most, such that by the actual *day* of new moon, the force was a small waxing one.

CHAPTER EIGHT

THE UNWANTED

COPING WITH SLUGS AND OTHER PESTS

Brief summary

* Slugs are the main leaf-pest of damp climates.
* Having clear space around the growing area is vital, to minimize accommodation for slugs.
* Pay special attention just after sowing and just after planting anything. Slugs love moisture and darkness, so keep surfaces clear of weeds, mulches and large objects, and avoid watering in the evening.
* Be prepared, in damp weather, to foray at dusk in search of invading or emerging molluscs.
* Have a look under larger leaves for slugs and snails sheltering, awaiting nightfall.
* Disposal is up to you; squashing underfoot or puncturing with a pointed knife saves any handling.
* Dry weather sees less damage but things can transform fast when the weather changes.
* Small-leaved, regularly picked salad plants are easier to keep slug-free than larger hearting specimens.
* Slug traps, barriers and nematodes all work to a point but require regular maintenance.
* Sowing seasonally is important, as plants are then stronger and more resistant to attack. This is especially true for avoiding most flea beetles.
* Aphids are seldom a serious problem because they have many predators such as ladybirds.

Blackfly aphids on beans arrive at the top.

There is no doubt about the main difficulty in growing many vegetables, and salad in particular. Hungry and slimy, they slither out in the damp and the dark, heading for tender leaves, YOUR tender leaves that you recently planted. When you go out in the morning, bare stalks of once promising plants await and you have to start again, with an extra month's wait for salad.

I have known that feeling so many times, more than enough to make me ask myself *every* time I sow or plant anything at all, "Is this going to grow away from slugs and snails?"

With the benefit of experience, I suffer few losses, and still learn some more about the behaviour patterns of slugs and other pests when plants *are* eaten. In this chapter I will pass on the lessons I have learnt so that you also have more chance of watching plants grow to fruition.

THE SLUG'S ROLE IN THE GARDEN

I never knew a garden without slugs and snails, yet growth is often still bountiful and healthy. So why are they there? What role do they have?

Waste disposal is their life's work, and difficulties arise for us when their understanding of waste does not agree with ours. Mostly they are clearing up decaying vegetation in less visible areas of darkness and moisture – quite helpful, really. But sometimes if the season is unusually wet they may breed excessively and need to expand their menu. Or we may sow or plant something weak, or at the wrong time, or in a

Large summer slug.

place where it will struggle. Slugs then receive the signal to go to work.

TRICKY TIMES

Timing is critical. The most difficult moments are always just after sowing and planting. Slugs love baby leaves and can eat a lot of them very quickly, clearing a potentially large harvest before, say, Venus has even set in the evening.

Slugs also have a feel for plants that are not happy and thriving, especially those that have been transplanted. The act of moving a plant definitely weakens it, and there is a critical period for about 10 days after planting when most of its energy is needed for settling in, making it less able to resist slimy nibbling. See pages 82-4 for tips on helping plants through these difficult days.

YOUR GROWING SITE

Slugs are all moisture and slime so they mostly live undercover or in damp crevices. Any walls, piles of stone, leafy bushes and overgrown areas are slug havens, and the further from them that you can situate your salad beds or containers, the safer your leaves will be.

It will also make a difference if you can manage a slug hunt to reduce their numbers, by looking under those loose stones and large leaves, in cracks of walls near the ground, and in any moist, shady area nearby. You'll soon become familiar with their favourite spots which new arrivals will always frequent – so regular checking is worthwhile, especially in damp weather.

Slugs of various descriptions. These were sheltering in the damp darkness afforded by the plank of wood.

WEATHER

It makes all the difference if dry conditions predominate, to the point that slugs seem to almost disappear. One relaxes. But they are able to lie dormant for long periods, and then reappear rapidly when it rains so that, suddenly, they are everywhere again. Should the weather stay wet for more than a fortnight in summer, slugs thrive and breeding is rapid As numbers increase and days remain damp, one has the unusual pleasure of seeing more of them by day. Through and just after any such wet spells in the growing period, regular patrols at dawn and dusk become important and are the most effective way I know of reducing numbers.

SLUG POISONS, TRAPS AND DETERRENTS

Synthetic slug pellets, usually of metaldehyde, work by drying the slugs' slime so that they grind to a halt and then shrivel. Such pellets are highly effective *and are needed in tiny amounts*, but unfortunately the affected slugs are then poisonous to birds, pets and hedgehogs that may eat them.

Some other slug pellets, described as organic and made of ferrous phosphate, work in a similar way and claim not to leave a poisoned slug, just a dry one. But I have found they do not prevent damage to leaves in seriously sluggy conditions, and I am not entirely happy about spreading all that iron and phosphorus on my garden. There is also a gel, which makes much the same anti-slug claims, but again I have not been impressed.

Nematodes that invade slugs' insides are more successful, but are expensive and relatively short-lived – after watering them on soil or compost, they are effective for about six to eight weeks. It may happen that you water them on at the beginning of what turns out to be a dry spring, in which case they are a waste of time and money. They are not a complete answer by any means.

A different approach is traps, filled with attractants that collect and imprison slugs. Home-made ones such as a jar of beer at soil level are just as effective as expensive offerings in shops and catalogues. But remember that they need more or less frequent disposal of their slimy contents and then refilling, meaning less beer for the gardener.

For container growing there are extra products, mostly based on copper and its minor electrical charge, which slugs dislike. You can buy copper-impregnated mats for pots to sit on and copper bands to attach around rims of containers. Neither will work if there are slugs or slug eggs in the container's compost already, or if a leaf grows over the top of the band and affords an entry passage to newly arriving slugs. Copper deterrents do not reduce slug numbers in your garden or patio, so they will be eating something elsewhere. Some athletic slugs have even been observed arching upwards and over the top of copper bands.

All of these so-called organic remedies and means of prevention need to be taken with a pinch of salt (also good

August – insect mesh over two-week-old plants: pak choi, kale, turnips.

Mesh pulled back shows no need to weed, thanks to no-dig soil.

at drying slugs out), and often require more effort than simply killing a few slugs at dusk or dawn.

SLUG DISPOSAL

If you are too squeamish to kill slugs, they need removing a long way from your garden and not too close to somebody else's! I feel it is better to acknowledge that we are talking life and death here – slugs' death or your plants' death. If your plants die, no crops will grow and you may be buying supermarket vegetables which, unless they are organic, will often have been grown in relatively lifeless soils and treated with some poisons. Even if organic they will be nothing like as fresh as your produce and will not give you the same life force as fresh salad from the garden. It seems to me much healthier all round to kill excess slugs, quickly and mercifully with a firm boot or sharp knife.

GETTING PLANTS UNDER-WAY SAFELY

Since most slug problems occur when seedlings are newly emerging and when plants are recently set out, you need to be extra vigilant at these times. I find April a rather nervous month, as so much new growth is just beginning, and certain other periods in the rest of the year when I have recently planted tender salads.

Aim to make your plants as tough as possible before planting out. Grow them as large as the modules / pots / seed trays and compost allow, give them three or four days of hardening off outside if

Pea shoots under fleece, 17 days after planting in April from a February sowing.

they have been raised indoors, and plant them in soil or compost that has been clear of weeds and surface debris for at least a fortnight beforehand.

Sow in season

Another sure way to better growth of young plants is by **sowing plants in season.** I can't say this too often, because so many seed packets offer vague information, encouraging sowing too early or too late.

There are many pointers elsewhere in this book on a balanced, seasonal approach to healthier growth. Two examples of what can happen if you sow at the wrong time will make this clearer:

* Sowing too early, before soil or compost has reached a high enough temperature for fast and vigorous growth, invites pests to eat. Lettuce may germinate outdoors in February, but will then almost certainly grow so slowly that one nibble by a passing slug will finish it off. Mizuna sown before July will rapidly flower and suffer many flea beetle holes.

* Sowing too late, such as spinach in September, results in weak growth and leaves full of slug holes.

Slug preferences

I did a trial of unseasonal salad and sowed Chinese cabbage in April. It was helped by rain in June to make a minimal heart, which I harvested just as it was turning into a flowering stem. But tucked inside the outer leaves were *seven* large orange slugs, while next to it was an endive with no slug holes or slimy inhab-

Mesh on hoops to protect lettuce and endive from rabbits.

itants. In other words, slugs have clear preferences, and when you grow healthy plants in season that are less interesting to them, you suffer less damage.

Pak choi provides another example. Whenever and wherever I grow it, there are always more slug holes than on nearby plants of different species. Only a late-summer sowing of pak choi has, in my experience, a chance of growing strongly and healthily enough to resist those almost inevitable nibbles.

A good growing medium

What you sow into makes a big difference as to whether slugs are interested or not. Out in the garden I find that well-composted, no-dig soil has a good chance of encouraging growth that is healthy and fast enough to resist occasional slug bites.

When growing in containers, use a good organic compost so that plants grow healthily and vigorously and are able to tolerate a few nibbles.

Keep harvesting, to help with weeds as well as slugs

Once your healthy, seasonal plants are growing strongly, you can look away briefly until they are offering leaves to pick in as little as two to three weeks from planting time. Regular picking of small-to-medium leaves will keep slugs to a minimum, compared with when there are older leaves edging towards decay, which offer pests a hiding place. Another reason for continual small harvests is weeds – large leaves can hide weed seedlings as well, so each picking

is an opportunity to remove any small weeds, which also helps to keep slug numbers down. Continual pulling of little weeds will soon clear soil of residual weed seeds so that it becomes simpler to grow nice crops.

OTHER PESTS

Apart from year-round slugs, most pests have particular seasons of prosperity and if you avoid these, your leaves will certainly be healthier. I also recommend that you accept small amounts of damage, because it is healthy for gardens to have a few pests, as this means there will be a background population of their predators.

Ants

Secretion of formic acid by ants eventually poisons roots, making leaves wilt as plants slowly die. Keeping soil moist in areas where they invade is an important deterrent, but this can be difficult along wooden edges of beds. I do not have a reliable answer here – boiling water is recommended by some, but it has not worked for me in beds where there is a huge mass of material to heat up, and I do not like its effect on worms either.

When you have weed-free paths, it's possible to have beds without sides. This reduces pest habitat, including ants.

Aphids

Here is an eloquent demonstration of why insecticide should be avoided, and a demonstration of how a balance between predator and prey is always

Pest prevention: Chinese cabbage need it, chicories less so.

Rabbit damage: they have nibbled some red mustard through the net.

Deer have eaten random rocket leaves.

too dry, or the plant is growing out of season. Aphid numbers can often be reduced with water alone, as they prefer dry leaves and plants, which are suffering some moisture stress.

Deer

Deer are almost impossible to fence out, and if they get into the habit of visiting your salad beds, there will be little left to eat. Their favourite salad leaves are chard, beets, endive and chicory: when browsing they either graze large pieces of outer leaves or snatch out the middles of plants. Use cloche hoops and black netting, weighted with stones at the side, to prevent deer browsing.

Flea beetles

These small, shiny, black, hopping insects are attracted only to brassica leaves – mustards, rocket, kale, pak choi and so forth (see Chapter 13). Their main season is spring and early summer, so later sowings in July and August are less affected, and leaves that grow in winter are especially clear of the little beetle holes.

Fleece or mesh can be used to reduce attacks by flea beetles, but it is easier to sow in season and grow non-brassica leaves in spring, which are of no interest to these beetles. The odd thing is that just one out-of-season rocket plant in the middle of many lettuces will somehow be noticed by them, and its leaves will soon be full of holes, especially in dry weather. As with aphids, watering reduces damage, but only marginally in the first half of the year.

evolving, yet is often invisible to us.

When scientists are studying aphids, and their aphid colonies start to diminish, they have a way of reviving them. **They kill them all by spraying aphicide!** This works because the poison kills all insects, the pests *and* their predators, but it is the aphids, that recolonize and proliferate most quickly.

In spring when I notice aphids on leaves and plants, I leave them alone because ladybirds usually arrive soon afterwards, whereupon the aphids diminish to insignificant levels. Only very occasionally do the aphids proliferate, for various reasons.

Severe infestations happen to plants that are unhealthy and are an indicator to the gardener that something is not quite right – for example, that the soil is

Rabbit damage to endive leaves – notice the holes, too.

Rabbits

Many rural gardens suffer from rabbits, and some fencing or netting will keep them out. However, they are not easy to deter, and if damage is severe, growing salad in containers near the house may be your only answer. UV-treated black polypropylene netting helps keep Homeacres rabbits at bay: we drape it over new plantings mostly, which rabbits damage more than large plants.

Root aphids

Tiny white or pale grey aphids often colonize lettuce roots during summer, and in dry summers especially can cause collapse of the plant or reduction of leaf size. I know of no remedy, but keeping soil or compost moist is a help (see page 32), as is growing other salads in late summer and autumn, when lettuce is out of season anyway.

Woodlice

Woodlice (also known as roly-polies, slaters and pill bugs) occasionally eat baby leaves and stems, especially of spinach. Letting hens loose in the garden will reduce their numbers and your crops. Best to avoid encouraging them by using less compost with woody pieces, their main food.

PART TWO

SALAD LEAF SEASONS OF HARVEST

CHAPTER NINE

LEAFING THROUGH THE SEASONS

CHANGING INGREDIENTS THROUGH THE YEAR

Salad leaves vary throughout the year. Their seasonal qualities can be separated into four overlapping yet quite different periods of harvest, which define the four salad seasons. Each one is characterized by its own spectrum of flavours and colours.

   The seasonal boundaries are not precise but offer a framework to better appreciate which plants to sow, grow and pick at different times of year. They are not intended as the last word and some extra sowings from outside this definition of seasons will sometimes work, especially when the weather is not seasonal! The average transition points are mid-April, mid-July, late September and early December. Winter is the longest season, requiring the most effort to grow leaves, but with harvests that are the most rewarding.

Charles planting peas for shoots in spring.

SPRING LEAVES FROM APRIL TO JULY

Brief summary of spring leaves

* There is a change to more numerous, larger and thicker leaves through these months.
* Lettuce grows healthily and strongly in spring, with even some hearts by mid-June.
* The other leafy staple of spring is true spinach, picked small.
* Wild rocket, from overwintered seedlings, maintains a pungent edge to spring salads.
* Sumptuous flavours can be grown, notably pea shoots, sorrel and various herbs.
* Other seasonal salad additions are flowering shoots, spring onions and asparagus.

Spring leaves are mostly of mild flavour and predominantly green, with a foundation of lettuce, spinach and chard, from overwintered plants and sowings in February (indoors) to May. Less abundant and more highly flavoured additions include bean and pea shoots, sorrel of different kinds, a little endive, herbs such as dill and coriander, and orache for a colour that is markedly more vivid than even the red lettuces. Other spring vegetables such as asparagus, radish and spring onions can liven up the salad bowl.

Spring is exciting – but it can also be a frustrating season. The poet Shelley observed optimistically, 'If winter comes, can spring be far behind?' This cuts both ways and when a biting north wind returns, one often reflects: *if spring comes, can winter be far behind?*

However, in spite of the two seasons overlapping frequently, two unalterable differences are a rapid increase in day length and sunlight that grows brighter. Light is vital for strong, healthy growth, and as the weeks pass it is a pleasure to notice the extra size, thickness and vigour of all salad leaves, as well as the arrival of different ones from more recently sown plants.

The leaves of April

The first leaves in early April are still wintry in character, almost entirely from overwintered plants such as **lamb's lettuce (corn salad), rocket** and some oriental greens such as **mibuna, mizuna, chards, endives, chicories, kales** and **lettuce.** There should also be worthwhile growth of leaves on perennial roots such as **sorrel,** and herbs such as **parsley, chervil** and **coriander.** Overwintered **lettuce** such as *Grenoble Red* may show signs of hearting.

But outdoor harvests in April are normally small and the first sowings of lettuce, mizuna and spinach, even if they were made indoors in January or February, will not usually make significant growth until early May.

Early spring is actually the best time for growing salad under cover, because glass or polythene structures benefit marvellously from the extra light, even becoming warm enough by day to keep out late frosts by night.

Spring lettuce just planted on 27 March gave 66kg (145lb 8oz) leaves over 13 weeks of picking.

Spring lettuce under fleece on a frosty morning.

Although April's frosts will not kill overwintered salad plants, which have endured far colder weather already, there can be some damage to their larger and slightly more tender leaves, and new growth will be checked. A covering of fleece is effective in bringing growth forward, except for slight damage to leaves where they are in contact with the freezing fabric.

Rapidly increasing day length encourages overwintered plants to switch from producing leaves to sending up a flower stem for production of seed. Endives are a good example: one minute they are, at last, developing a tempting-looking heart; then a week later this heart is transforming into a more bitter stem. Lamb's lettuce likewise, after cropping well in early April, quickly develops pretty and very small pale blue flowers after mid-month, which can be eaten but are not substantial.

The productive life of some salad plants can be extended by pinching out all flowering stems, and by frequent harvests. Regular picking of an endive's outer leaves can stimulate the growth of new leaves for up to a month longer. Rocket and chards will obligingly return to leaf creation when their stems are removed, with the side effect that new leaves are smaller, stronger in flavour and slightly more bitter.

Some salad plants reserve the best flavour and sweetness for their **flowering shoots –** brassicas such as kale, whose stems and flower buds are one of early spring's most tempting offerings. Oriental leaves such as mizuna and mibuna send up long, thin stalks with yellow flowers that are both pretty and deliciously sweet. And after mid-month comes the tastiest stem of all as the first spears of **asparagus** push upwards – eaten raw, they are crunchy, sweet and slightly salty as well.

All in all, April's leaves and flowers, although quite scarce, have some of the year's most varied flavours, and can really lift one's mood after winter.

The leaves of May

May patrols the boundary between winter scarcity and summer riches, with fluctuating temperatures that are so unpredictable. By the month's end, if not before, your first sowings of many different leaves should be offering regular meals.

A raised bed such as those shown in Chapter 3 can make a huge difference here because its compost will warm up more reliably than garden soil, which risks remaining cold in a wet spring. Containers and window boxes offer similar benefits of extra warmth.

Lettuces love the bright but not too hot conditions at this time of year, and they are usually the most common leaf in May salad bowls. The wide range of lettuce varieties affords opportunities to bring vibrant colours and textures to both your garden and table. Picking the outer leaves off well-spaced plants, or cutting leaves in more thickly sown rows, brings the harvest forward by at least a month, instead of waiting until June for the first lettuce hearts.

Spinach is another staple in May, with an especially appealing crunch to its first succulent leaves before they

Winter-season spinach and chervil, netted against pests.

Winter purslane, land cress, *Red Dragon* mustard, and lamb's lettuce in January.

grow thinner with age. In warm weather spinach grows rapidly and can be picked every other day to keep its leaves small. **Wild rocket** from overwintered plants grows strongly in May, on plants that overwintered after sowing in September. Keep cutting to encourage new growth and less flowering.

There is a small window of opportunity, mainly in early May, for some useful oriental leaves, if they are sown early enough. I sow **mizuna** indoors in February and plant it out in late March, preferably under fleece, to have two or three cuts before it flowers and before too many flea beetles arrive. **Komatsuna** is another possibility, with somewhat larger leaves. **Sorrel** should be abundant in May, initially from plants established the year before and then from new sowings in March. A few small leaves bring zest and bite to more watery lettuce, as do the last pickings of overwintered **chervil** and **parsley**. **Coriander** is more rapid to establish and March sowings can offer small bundles of powerful taste, when a few leaves are gathered off small plants.

Vibrant colour is provided by the odd plant of **orache**, while **spring onions** are growing well in May and can be one of the month's staples. Other options for livening up May salads include **chives** and **garlic chives** for tangy onion flavours and **chive flowers** for both taste and colour.

An exotic, delicious idea is to use the first **pea shoots**, whose regular picking encourages more to appear, all bringing a sweet taste of pea at a time of year when it is most welcome (see Chapter 15, pages 186–7).

Spinach *Red Bordeaux F1.*

The leaves of June

By June there should be no shortage of leaves, and lettuce has really come into its own – this is probably its best month for rapid growth, glossy leaves and absence of mildew. **Leaf lettuce** can be gathered all month from plants sown in late winter, whose longevity is improved by picking rather than cutting. Many varieties offer a leaf per day at this time of year, although dark red ones are a little slower. Some of the more vigorous ones, such as *Solstice,* may rise to flower before the month's end.

Alternatively, by mid-June the first **lettuce hearts**, such as *Little Gem,* should be forming and they are a sweet temptation to grace any meal. Hearting cos and crisp lettuce mature a little later so a few of each sort is a way of spreading the season and avoiding gluts. Cutting lettuce hearts is not terminal to the plant, as some new leaves should appear out of the remaining stump, but their growth is not usually significant, and regular sowing is the main option if you like hearts more than leaves.

March sowings of **spinach** and **chard** will start rising to flower in June so they are best resown in May. Pinching out their flowering stems will prolong picking time, but the flavour of new sowings is better.

Some bitter tastes and firmer textures come from overwintered **wild rocket**, now growing more pungent by the day. Also from April sowings of **endives**, which can be treated like leaf lettuce and whose outer leaves can be picked on a regular basis. There is even a pale yellow endive (*Bianca Riccia da Taglio*), which is pleasantly bright and uplifting in the garden (see Chapter 12).

Tall **spring onions** look nice in the garden and can be harvested all month. The green leaf of freshly pulled onions is much tastier than that of shop-bought ones, and you have the choice of whether to pick them small or large.

June has strong herbal possibilities, especially **dill**, a few sprigs of which give a wonderfully clean aroma to salad. Floral options increase through the month, such as **coriander, pot marigold, borage, heartsease** and **pea flowers.**

SUMMER LEAVES FROM JULY TO SEPTEMBER

Brief summary of summer leaves

* Salads become more and more varied through the summer.
* Lettuce is gradually augmented with any or all of endives, chicories and oriental leaves.
* Stronger tastes appear and many aromatic herby flavours are possible.

Summer leaves are sown during May, June and July, and are still mostly lettuce, but with different herbs such as basil. Texture and flavour is offered by summer sowings such as purslane. There can also be hearting endives by July, radicchio hearts by August and the first oriental leaves and rocket by early September. Colour variations come from red amaranth and basil, red lettuce, yellow endives and various

Savoy cabbage interplanted between lettuce in summer.

shades of chicory. Strong flavours may be introduced with some bitter chicory and endive leaves, and chard is a reliable background addition. Summer has aspects of both spring and autumn, while two of its signature flavours are basil and purslane.

The character of leaf harvests can swing back and forth throughout the summer, as growth is so rapid and there is an increasing choice of salad plants to grow. A typical early July salad is as much spring as summer, and a September one can be quite autumnal, depending on what you sowed. The following is an outline of salad essence as it unfolds through summer.

The leaves of early July

Most **leaf lettuce** sown in late winter or early spring should crop until mid-July or so, at which point a late-May sowing will be a good replacement and should crop through July and most of August. If you want **hearted lettuce**, sow a few seeds every three weeks until mid-July.

Endives become more prominent from now on, and leaf endives sown from early June can offer leaves throughout summer. They are useful if you suffer root aphid on lettuce in summer. **Leaf chicories** are another somewhat bitter option, or *Palla Rossa* **varieties** can be sown in June for **hearting** from late August; their heart leaves are crunchy, bittersweet and of vibrant colour.

Blood-veined sorrel looks great but has a bitter flavour.

Spring sowings of **sorrel, dill, coriander** and even **parsley** tend to start flowering through July so more sowings are needed by early summer. In hot weather, or in an indoor growing space, the summer's top and most consistent flavour is **basil**. When regularly picked and with all flowering shoots removed, most basil will grow steadily until night temperatures drop in September or October. It really does not like cool, damp weather so a typical British summer is not ideal for growing outdoors, unless you have a really sheltered, sunny spot. Look at Chapter 16, pages 195-8 for an idea of all the basil flavours you can grow.

For extra red colour, orache is now replaced by *Garnet Red* **amaranth,** whose dark, ruby leaves also look attractive in the garden.

The leaves of late July and early August

Through this peak of summer, leaves are tending to gain in flavour as the first **rocket** and a few **mizuna** leaves become available. With the leaves that are already growing, this is a time of great and increasing salad variety and quantity, as leaves grow fast in warmth and long days.

One leaf to avoid in summer is **spinach**, whose flowering season lasts through June and July, so it's good to resow in early August. A delicious alternative, in dry summers especially, is **purslane** (not the winter purslane which should really be called claytonia). It thrives in hot sun and has fleshy, rounded and succulent leaves, which

Seeding lettuce in late summer: *Winter Density, Lollo Rossa, Bijou.*

add a welcome bite to the salad bowl in hot summers but less so in wet ones when its growth is stunted.

The leaves of late August and September

These six weeks are a time of major evolution in leaf salads. **Lettuce** begins to run into problems. With longer nights and damper days, it becomes prone to mildew on leaves, whose size and thickness start to decrease. Dry weather lessens the risk of mildew but can make lettuce more vulnerable to root aphids, so it becomes less of a staple.

In its place, **oriental leaves** and **salad rocket** are useful. Any looming gaps in salad supply can be filled with sowings of **mizuna** and **leaf radish**, probably the fastest growers, as well as various types of **mustards, pak choi, mibuna** and other less well-known varieties (see Chapter 13). **Spinach** is back in season, although slugs may damage its leaves in wet weather.

Chicories are forming pretty hearts of **red radicchio** and **sugarloaf**. The former have utterly beautiful patterns of red and white to their heart-leaves, while the latter are much paler and thinner, of unremarkable flavour but a useful base for other, stronger flavours, such as **basil** which should still be growing. **Dill** and **coriander** are productive now, from sowings in high summer.

Endives also start to reveal their best qualities in late summer, and should make large, attractive and slightly blanched hearts of sweeter leaves than their outer green ones. **Scarole endives**, with flat, soft and broad leaves, make especially tasty hearts that stand reasonably well, unlike the hearts of most **frizzy endives** which tend to rot soon after they are fully developed. Two or three sowings in July and into early August are necessary for a continuity of hearting endives through late summer and onwards.

A leaf which improves in quality through this period is rocket, partly because it has less flea-beetle holes and partly because it often becomes larger and fleshier in mild, damp weather as opposed to dry heat. *Red Russian* **kale** is another attractive and tender brassica leaf for late summer.

By September's end, the main season of rapid leaf production is drawing to a close, apart from a few notable exceptions described below.

AUTUMN LEAVES FROM OCTOBER TO DECEMBER

Brief summary of autumn leaves

* Leaves decrease in size until January.
* Autumn can still be an abundant time for salads, much more than in winter.
* Quantities, colours and tastes can be increased by using hearted chicories.
* Flavours become stronger and slightly more bitter.

Leaves sown in July and August are of a stronger or more bitter flavour, and less aromatic. Lettuce loses its central role to oriental leaves, rocket, chicories and endives. Lamb's lettuce (corn salad) and winter purslane offer a mild and soft counterbalance, or you may prefer using land cress to increase the bite. Chards, spinach and parsley diminish through autumn and have much smaller leaves by November. Many shades of green, from dark rocket to the pale, creamy sugarloaf, can be complemented by a range of pink and red chicory hearts and leaves.

Generally speaking, leaves in the winter are precious and to treasure, having extra appeal in meals that tend to become more starchy and dense. Is it their smallness and scarcity that makes them taste better, or is it some concentration of flavour as a result of slower growth? Or is it that plants with an ability to survive cold weather and low light levels are also possessed of special qualities that translate as top taste and healthy vitality in our winter salads? Grow some for yourself and see what you think. It is harder work than in spring and summer, but rewarding.

The leaves of October

All through October there is a massive slowdown of growth as light wanes and temperatures drop, especially after any early frost. Just occasionally a spell of Indian summer weather will prolong growth, but such warmth is a bonus and not to be relied upon. Even in mild autumns it is striking how the relatively numerous new leaves are much smaller, making harvests less abundant.

As a result, it becomes useful to have some hearted plants available for creating larger bowls of salad, or for continual top-ups. **Hearts of endives**, **chicories** and **Chinese cabbage** are of top quality at this time of year and have crunchy leaves of many different flavours. They can be picked fresh or stored in a cool, damp place, their leaves peeled off as required.

Herbs become scarcer: **parsley** survives well in cooler weather but is slow-growing unless you have an indoor space for it. **Coriander** and **chervil** are good for winter flavour. These herbs withstand most frost but do not like continual rain and wind.

The leaves of November and December

From late November until March, it is only true winter plants that make worthwhile leaves, and then only in mild weather of temperatures around 10°C (50°F) by day and minimal frost by night: **lamb's lettuce (corn salad), winter purslane, land cress, chicories, endives, salad rocket, mustards, mizuna, leaf radish** and other **oriental leaves**.

Some **parsley, chard** and **spinach** may still grow a little, while any **lettuce leaves** and **endive hearts** will probably be of poor quality, with mildew causing leaves to rot.

Radicchios and **sugarloaves** are usually the only hearts to survive some frost and will be a joy to find, sometimes hidden under a thin layer of rotten foliage. Removal of all old chicory leaves when harvesting hearts will

Autumn: second and third plantings include kales, mustards and *Kaibroc* broccoli.

clear space for new growth of baby leaves out of the same root in late winter and early spring.

Hearts that have been stored, such as **Chinese cabbage**, can be defoliated as needed, but are unlikely to stay healthy beyond Christmas. Chicories grown for forcing need digging up before Christmas and setting to grow in a dark place, to have **chicons** in the new year (see Chapter 12, pages 150–3).

WINTER LEAVES FROM DECEMBER TO APRIL

Brief summary of winter leaves

*   Cold winters see little new growth.
*   In mild winters, lamb's lettuce, land cress and winter purslane grow slowly and surely.
*   Rocket, mizuna, mustards, leaf radish, leaf chicory, kale and spinach also contribute a little.
*   Outdoor leaves in winter are scarce; some indoor growing is worthwhile.

Mostly from sowings in late August and September, harvests of winter leaves are usually scarce and small, yet often have the greatest variety of taste and texture. Their slow-grown leaves are robust, possessing a lower proportion of water that allows them to cope with being frozen. They include lamb's lettuce (corn salad), mustards, rocket, winter purslane, land cress, kales, leaf chicories, leaf endives and perhaps a few forced chicons. In mild winters there can also be some mizuna and sweet spinach leaves. To cheer us up, it is possible to enjoy a warming range of colour, including red mustard and bright yellow chicons.

The leaves of January and February

These are the leanest months for outdoor picking. Even if a cloche or fleece is used to cover plants, little *significant* growth will happen; instead plants should suffer less damage from wind, frost and rain, yield just occasional leaves and then be in good shape for new growth in late winter and early spring. The most likely plants to offer new leaves at this time are **rocket, mustards, leaf radish,** and to a lesser extent **chicories, spinach** and **chard**.

The jewel in the crown of winter salads, however, is **lamb's lettuce (corn salad)** which can grow a surprising amount in mild spells of weather. Having said that, you would need a lot of lamb's lettuce to fill the salad bowl regularly because its leaves are quite small, and they are also fiddly to pick.

Indoor-forced **chicons** are a welcome standby, for their bright yellow colour and buttery bittersweet taste. Growth can be regulated by moving pots or bags of chicory roots to warmer or colder places indoors.

The leaves of March

All the January and February leaves continue, and harvests off the same

Tatsoi *Rozetto F1* in November. It was sown mid-August and has given many harvests.

plants increase in size and weight as daylight returns. Depending on the weather, some worthwhile **spinach** and **lettuce** leaves may be had towards the month's end. The onion family make welcome appearances as overwintered **spring onions**, from sowings in August, start to bulk up, and **chives** may attain a harvestable size.

March can be a frustrating time because longer days put one in the mood for spring foods, and outdoor leaves are often still quite scarce. It is one of the best months for growing leaves under cover, where glass or plastic will multiply the sun's new energy and enable worthwhile growth of **oriental leaves, rocket, spinach, lettuce, endives, chicories, chard** and some **herbs**. See Chapter 19 for more details.

CHAPTER TEN

RECIPES FOR ALL SEASONS

LEAFY MEALS MONTH BY MONTH

One joy of salads is that they offer such varied combinations of colour, flavour and texture, making for successful salad meals that are based on the skill of the gardener as much as of the cook.

The main way we eat salad is as a seasonal mixture of leaves, 10 or more kinds in a bowl together, just on their own. The mix changes almost completely with each season, allowing appreciation and enjoyment of those flavours, from the fragrance of spring pea shoots and summer basil to the pungency of winter mustards.

Salad leaves also lend themselves to the creation of many more dishes, often in combination with other seasonal ingredients, and we hope you will enjoy some of the suggestions here. Steph and I have assembled the simple recipes for our favourite salads. Feel free to alter the leaf mix according to your seasonal harvests.

September: Charles tidies tatsoi and Chinese cabbage.

SPRING RECIPES
Dressing for spring salads

Spring leaves, being mostly mild, green and tender, are well complemented by this variation of classic vinaigrette, which has the added flavour of nut or seed oils and is spiced up with mustard:

4 tbsp olive oil
1-2 tbsp walnut or toasted sesame oil
1 tbsp cider or wine vinegar
2 tsp wholegrain mustard
salt and pepper to taste

Shake all the ingredients together in a bottle or jar and use immediately

Inner leaves (clockwise from top): leaf radish, cress *Cressida*, green purslane

The flavours are mild and varied – use only a little dressing to complement them.

APRIL
Salad of micro leaves

These baby leaves were grown in two seed trays in a greenhouse and cut with a knife, three and a half weeks after being sown in late March. There was little regrowth because the stems were cut through.
Outer leaves (clockwise from top):
Mizuna
Komatsuna
Mustard, *Golden Streaks*
Kale, *Nero di Toscana*
Amaranth, *Garnet Red*
Rocket
Ruby Chard, *Charlotte*
Spinach, *Tetona* (equivalent to *Lazio*)
Beet, *Red Titan*
Yellow chard

MAY
Whole roasted lettuce salad with nettle pesto

This recipe combines homegrown overwintered lettuce with fresh foraged shoots of spring nettles. The addition of sunflower and pumpkin seeds makes this simple salad a delicious main course, served with crusty bread.

1 whole firm, crunchy lettuce such as *Grenoble Red*
olive or sunflower oil
1 tbsp cider vinegar

1 tbsp sunflower seeds
1 tbsp pumpkin seeds

Pesto
125g (4½ oz) nettle tops
100g (3½ oz) sunflower seeds
100g (3½ oz) pumpkin seeds
125ml (4½fl oz) olive or sunflower oil
juice of ½ lemon
2-3 cloves garlic, peeled
salt and pepper

Preheat the oven to 180°C (350°F / Gas Mark 4)

Cut the lettuce into quarters and place in an oven dish. Drizzle over a little oil and the cider vinegar. Sprinkle the seeds on top and roast in the oven until cooked, 15-20 minutes.

Meanwhile, prepare the pesto. Spread the seeds across a baking tray. Toast them in the oven, checking every few minutes to make sure they don't burn. Remove after 5 minutes or so and allow to cool.

Steam the nettle tops, cool and then place in a blender with the seeds, oil, lemon juice, garlic and a little salt and pepper. Process until everything has been puréed, adding a little water if necessary. Season according to taste.

Arrange the roasted lettuce on a dish, drizzle some of the pesto over the top and serve with crusty bread.

Spicy spinach, spring salad and potato cakes

4 medium sized potatoes, peeled and diced
salt and pepper
vegetable oil for frying
1 medium-sized onion, finely chopped
1 tsp finely chopped chillies (more if you like it spicy)
2 cloves garlic, finely chopped
1 tsp finely chopped ginger
½ tsp ground cumin
½ tsp ground coriander
1 tsp garam masala
100g (3½ oz) spinach, finely chopped
100g (3½ oz) spring salad leaves, finely chopped
3 tsp chickpea flour

Place the potatoes in a saucepan, cover with boiling water, add a pinch of salt and boil until soft. Remove from the heat and strain. Mash, then set aside.

Heat a little oil into a heavy pan, add the onions, chillies, garlic and ginger and fry over a low heat until the onion is transparent.

Add the spices and cook for another minute, then add the spinach and salad leaves, salt and pepper. Stir until the leaves are wilted and cooked through, then remove from the heat.

Add the chickpea flour and stir through the mixture, then add the mashed potato, combining thoroughly.

Allow to cool.

Once cool, divide the mixture equally and shape into patties. Shallow fry in hot oil, turning once, until cooked through.

Serve with chutneys and fresh salad leaves.

Lettuce leaves with spring onion, asparagus and baby amaranth

In May I harvested the leaves of *Mottistone*, *Grenoble Red*, *Bijou* and *Bergamo*, which were grown in a window box to make this dish.

leaves from 4 lettuce plants
4 asparagus spears, blanched for 2 minutes
4 spring onions, peeled and trimmed
sprinkling of colourful baby leaves, in this case amaranth

Wash, shake dry and lay out the lettuce. Arrange the asparagus and spring onion on top, as well as the few tiny leaves of amaranth.

Serve with a vinaigrette. Mayonnaise or creamy garlic dressing is delicious for dipping the asparagus and spring onion too.

JUNE

Spring risotto with sugar peas and pea shoots

This is a useful recipe if your sugar snap peas have escaped your notice and the pods have become too coarse to eat. You need not waste the pods; they can be boiled for stock or soup.

200g (7 oz) risotto rice
1 onion or 3-4 shallots
2-3 cloves of garlic
olive oil
salt and pepper
100ml (3½fl oz) cider (or white wine)
500ml (18fl oz) vegetable stock
handful of broad beans
handful of peas – sugar snap or

'normal' garden peas

Soak the rice in cold water for 20 minutes.

Peel and chop the onions or shallots and garlic.

Pour 2 tbsp (or more if needed) olive oil into an ovenproof pan. Add the onions and garlic and sauté until soft.

Drain the rice and add to the onions. Season with salt and pepper.

Pour in the cider, followed by the stock. When it has come to the boil, cover and put in the oven on a low heat for about 30 minutes.

Meanwhile, pod the broad beans and the coarser peas.

After 30 minutes, check how liquid the risotto is. Add some water if it becomes too dry and transfer the pan to the top of the stove.

Add the broad beans and peas, cover and briefly steam on the surface of the risotto. Remove the pan lid and let any surplus liquid boil away.

Remove the pan from the stove.

Serve with vegetables of the season, in this case steamed sugar snaps in their pods and a side salad of raw pea shoots, with a drizzle of garlic mustard dressing. Simply arrange the shoots on the side of the plate.

SUMMER RECIPES
Dressing for summer salads

Summer flavours are extremely varied and include many possibilities for eating vegetables raw. Garlic comes ready in early July and fresh garlic is milder than winter garlic. Vary the amount of garlic in this recipe according to your preference – we like garlic! This dressing is delicious with finely chopped fresh herbs added to the mix too.

4-6 cloves fresh garlic, peeled and finely chopped
1 tbsp Dijon mustard
juice of ½ lemon
2 tbsp cider or wine vinegar
100ml (3½fl oz) olive oil
salt and pepper

Either place all the ingredients into a jug and whisk or, for a smoother dressing, place everything in a blender and whizz until processed.

JULY

Lettuce heart opened out, with roasted beetroot salad

A whole hearted lettuce such as *Marvel of Four Seasons* makes a fantastic base for any dish, left intact here and splayed open from the top. Washing is more difficult than with individual leaves and needs some care; after washing hold it gently upside down to shake out the water.

If you don't have a hearted lettuce, a base of mixed seasonal leaves is just as delicious.

1 hearted lettuce
2 medium beetroot, any colour
2 onions
4 stalks celery
olive oil
125g (4½ oz) walnuts

Preheat the oven to 180°C (350°F / gas mark 4)

Chop the beetroot, onion and celery into smallish pieces (around 1.5cm / ½"). Spread them out on an oven dish and drizzle over olive oil. Mix well with your hands and roast in the oven for around 30 minutes. After 15 minutes,

mix in the walnuts.

Either serve the vegetables on top of the lettuce while hot, which softens the leaves, or allow them to cool first. Be sure to scrape all of those pan juices onto the vegetables.

Season to taste if you wish.

Green soup

This soup is great for using up surplus leaves, and can be made with different leaves at any time of the year when harvests are bountiful. It can be eaten hot or cold.

2 large or 4 medium-sized onions
6 small cloves garlic
2 stalks of celery
olive oil
6 medium–large potatoes
2 pints vegetable stock
salt & pepper
30 or so large leaves of leaf radish, pak choi, mizuna or equivalent
30 or so lettuce leaves
20 leaves of spinach, chard and herbs

Chop the onions, garlic and celery and add to a large pan with a good drizzle of olive oil.

Peel and slice the potatoes, then add to the pan. Add the vegetable stock, season and bring to the boil. Simmer for 30 minutes.

Turn off the heat.

Chop the leaves, add to the pan and stir. Allow the leaves to wilt for 2-3 minutes, then purée with a hand-held blender.

Taste, season to taste and serve.

AUGUST

French bean salad with sorrel and French tarragon

3 tbsp olive oil
juice and zest of ½ lemon
2 spring onions, finely chopped
1 tsp wholegrain mustard
4 tsp fresh French tarragon, finely
   chopped
1 clove garlic, finely chopped

salt and pepper
500g (1lb 2oz) French beans, any
   kind, topped and tailed
small bunch of sorrel, chopped

Optional:
flaked almonds

First, make the dressing by combining all the ingredients (other than the beans and sorrel). Taste and season.

Boil the beans until just cooked, then pour into a colander in the sink and quickly cool by running cold water over them. Pour into a bowl, add the dressing and sorrel, and mix carefully.

Decorate with almonds if you wish.

Summer salad with edible flowers

A simple recipe of beautiful colours, varied textures and a good range of flavours, using whatever leaves and flowers you have grown.

1 tbsp cider vinegar
3 tbsp olive oil
1 tbsp lemon juice
salt and pepper to taste
2 carrots
2 medium yellow beetroot
125g (14.5oz) cashew nuts
salad leaves
edible flowers (e.g. heartsease,
   nasturtium, calendula, gem
   marigold, borage)

First, make the vinaigrette by combining the cider vinegar, olive oil, lemon juice and seasoning.

Grate the carrots and beetroot, place in a mixing bowl and add the cashew nuts. Pour over the salad dressing and combine thoroughly.

Arrange the salad leaves in a serving dish. Spoon on the carrot salad and arrange the edible flowers on top.

Green herb houmous and lettuce wraps

Houmous:
300g (10½oz) cooked chickpeas (plus the cooking liquid)
4 tsp tahini
juice of ½ lemon
25g green leafy herbs (e.g. basil, coriander, dill, parsley, sorrel)
2 cloves chopped garlic
2 tbsp olive oil
Salt and pepper

Lettuce and fillings:
Large lettuce leaves
raw seasonal vegetables (e.g. carrot, cucumber, celery, cabbage, turnip, kohl rabi)

To make the houmous, place the chickpeas, tahini, lemon juice, herbs, garlic, olive oil, seasoning and 100ml (3½fl oz) of the cooking liquid into the blender. Process, adding a little more cooking liquid if required (if you have no liquid, use water). Transfer to a serving dish.

Use a mandolin or sharp knife to cut the vegetables into thin strips. Arrange them on a platter with the lettuce leaves. To assemble the wraps, take a lettuce leaf, spread some hummus across the middle, add vegetables and roll up.

SEPTEMBER

Lime basil, courgette and fennel salad

1 handful lime basil leaves (or whatever basil you have)
juice ½ lemon
4 tbsp olive oil
1 tbsp cider vinegar
salt and pepper to taste
1 green courgette
1 yellow courgette (or two green ones)
2 fennel bulbs
salad leaves

First, make the dressing by placing the basil leaves, lemon juice, oil and vinegar in a blender, whizzing until everything is combined. Taste and season.

With a sharp knife or mandolin, thinly slice the courgettes and fennel bulbs.

Place in a bowl, drizzle over the salad dressing and mix carefully.

Serve with fresh seasonal leaves.

Cucumber, cashew nuts and pumpkin seeds on a bed of dark red lettuce, garnished with red nasturtium flowers

The colours in this salad are breathtaking, and the flavours are excellent too! The flowers add a zest of extra taste and vibrant colour, especially if you have *Empress of India* nasturtium

1 large or 2 small cucumbers
1 tbsp salt
lettuce leaves, darkly coloured
   (e.g. *Rosemoor, Bijou, Redina,*
   ***Nymans* or *Foxley*)**
2-3 tbsp cashew nuts, plain or
   roasted
1 tbsp pumpkin seeds

Slice the cucumbers and sprinkle with salt.

An hour or so later, drain off the water which has been drawn out, enhancing the cucumber's sweetness and digestibility. Pat dry.

Pick and wash the lettuce leaves, and arrange them around a medium to large plate.

Lay the slices of cucumber in a circle around the outside of the plate, on top of the leaves.

Make a small mound of cashew nuts in the middle, preferably whole ones, then have some fun decorating the cucumber with pumpkin seeds.

AUTUMN RECIPES

Dressing for autumn salads

Since autumn's leaves have stronger and more bitter flavours, some sweetening of a dressing with balsamic vinegar, muscovado sugar or honey provides a nice balance, and milder oils work better at this time of year.

5 tbsp sunflower or olive oil
1 tbsp balsamic vinegar (best quality)
1-2 tsp sugar or clear honey
1 tsp wholegrain mustard
salt and pepper to taste

Shake all the ingredients vigorously in a jar or bottle, making sure the sweeteners have dissolved.

OCTOBER

Whole scarole endive and croutons

It feels extravagant to use a whole heart in one salad, but the effect is so rich and the taste of the tender heart leaves is so fine that plates keep getting re-filled.

1 whole scarole endive
4 slices of wholemeal bread
(homemade if you can)
2 tbsp olive oil
1 sweet pepper (any colour), cut into strips
1-2 cloves garlic, finely chopped

Cut across the base of the endive to free up its leaves, then discard the outer green ones (this is optional – you may enjoy their more bitter flavour).

Wash and drain, cut all leaves into about 2cm (1") lengths then place in a bowl.

Trim the crusts off the bread and cut into about 1cm (½") cubes.

Fry in the oil for about 5 minutes until golden or dark brown (depending on the bread), add to the chopped endive.

Garnish with strips of pepper and scatter garlic over the top.

There is no need for dressing here as there is oil and salt in the bread.

Roasted chicory and autumn vegetable salad

1 whole chicory or radicchio of your choice
3 carrots
1 medium sized red or yellow beetroot
1 medium uchiki kuri squash (or butternut), seeds removed*
2-3 potatoes
2 turnips, peeled
2 onions (red or white) or 2 leeks
(use any other autumn vegetables that you fancy!)
*Uchiki kuri does not need peeling, but other squash usually do.

Preheat the oven to 180°C (350°F / gas mark 4)

Wash the chicory or radicchio, then cut into quarters.

Wash the carrots, beetroot, squash, potatoes and turnips and cut into approx. 3cm (1") cubes.

Peel and dice the onions.

Arrange everything in a roasting tin, drizzle with olive on and a sprinkle of salt (if desired), and place in the oven for 30 minutes. After 15 minutes, check to make sure nothing is sticking and that they are roasting well.

Serve with seasonal salad leaves or steamed green vegetables.

RECIPE IDEAS

Before the dark days set in too insistently, why not enjoy a leafy harvest festival in the last mild days, when many summer leaves linger and those of autumn are still growing at a reasonable pace.

On one plate you could arrange, for example, pak choi *Hanakan F1*, tatsoi and mustard *Ruby Streaks*, all at their prime and quite different in colour and taste. Their brassica flavour makes them suitable in dishes where cabbage would normally be served.

Another possibility in autumn is to make a mix of all different sorts of leaves, including mustards, sorrels, many oriental leaves, rockets, various lettuces, frizzy endives and even some final leaves of basil. The range of possible leaves is awesome at this time of year, and there are still flowers for decoration as well.

WINTER RECIPES

Dressing for winter salads

Many winter leaves are strong and bitter so the autumn dressing clothes them nicely, or try this ginger salad dressing

3 tbsp olive oil
1 tbsp cider vinegar
1 clove minced garlic
1 tsp minced fresh ginger
1 tsp maple syrup (or honey)
1 tbsp tamari or soy sauce
chopped herbs to taste

Place all of the ingredients together in a jug, small bowl or blender and mix together.

DECEMBER

Radicchio in hot balsamic vinegar

Radicchio hearts can be harvested when mature and kept in a cool place or the fridge until needed. Their pretty leaves – whether red *Palla Rossa* or *Treviso* or green *Lusia* – need just enough time in the pan to soak up the balsamic vinegar's sweet and sour tastes, becoming denser and more richly flavoured in the process. They are well complemented by a scattering of crisp, raw Chinese cabbage or endive leaves.

2 tbsp olive oil
2 tbsp balsamic vinegar
2 cloves garlic, finely chopped
Approx. 350g (12½oz) small whole radicchio leaves
A few small leaves of Chinese cabbage or endive heart

Heat the oil and vinegar, add the garlic and cook for about 1 minute.

Add the radicchio leaves – but only briefly, for 2 minutes or less, so that they just collapse a little and retain their colour. Any longer and they turn to brown mush – which happens quickly!

Scatter the small, pale heart leaves on top for a striking contrast of colour and texture.

JANUARY/FEBRUARY

Tastes of winter

A simple combination of superb winter flavours.

approx 2 handfuls of winter purslane and lamb's lettuce
1 apple, chopped (in this case I used Ellisons Orange)
2-3 celery stalks, sliced
10 walnuts, freshly shelled

Wash and rinse the leaves.

A dressing is optional, as there is so much oil and flavour in freshly shelled walnuts.

MARCH

Bean salad with roasted red onions, tomatoes and leaves, and a balsamic dressing

This salad combines overwintered homemade dried tomatoes with onions and fresh spring leaves. It is good to make at any time of year, when the flavours change with the different salads available.

80g (2¾ oz) home-saved *Czar* runner beans or borlotti beans (makes 240g/8½oz) cooked
handful of homemade dried

tomatoes, or shop-bought
4 red onions, thinly sliced
2 cloves garlic, thinly sliced
olive oil
seasonal mixed salad leaves
Dressing:
balsamic vinegar
3tbsp olive oil
reserved tomato liquid
salt and pepper to taste

Soak the beans overnight in plenty of water. Drain and put in a pan well covered with water. Bring to the boil, reduce to a simmer and cook for 30 minutes or so until tender. Drain and allow to cool.

Soak the tomatoes in a little warm water to soften. Drain, reserving the soaking liquid for the salad dressing.

Meanwhile, fry the onions in a pan

with a good glug of olive oil over a low heat until transparent. Allow to cool.

Place the salad leaves in a bowl and add the beans, onions and tomatoes. Make a salad dressing using 1 tbsp balsamic vinegar, 3 tbsp olive oil, the tomato liquid and season to taste. Pour the dressing over the salad, mix together and serve.

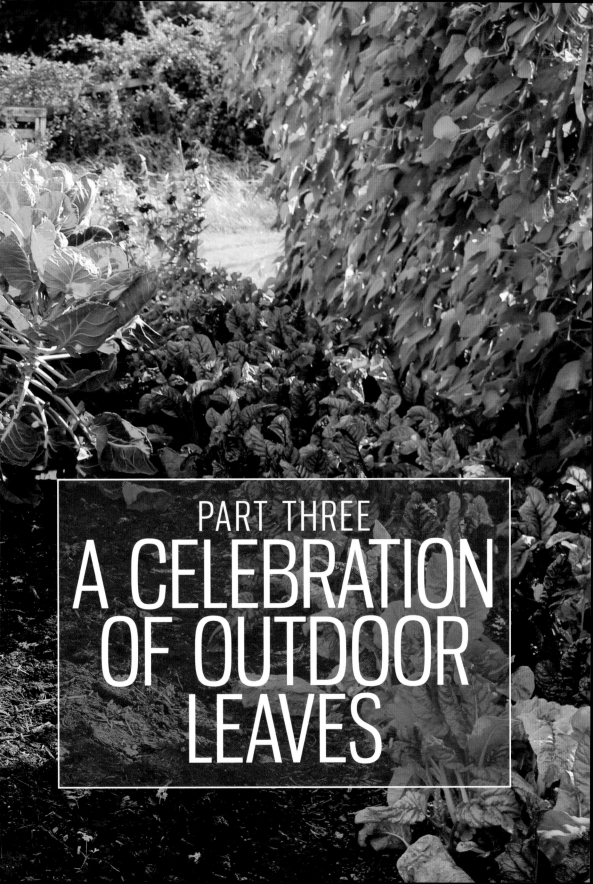

PART THREE
A CELEBRATION OF OUTDOOR LEAVES

CHAPTER ELEVEN

LETTUCE

FAST-GROWING, PLENTIFUL LEAVES

Brief summary

* Best sown indoors from January to August.
* Best sown outdoors from March to August.
* Main season of outdoor harvest: May to October.
* Choose between picking leaves regularly or allowing hearts to form.
* Regular picking of lettuce gives probably the highest yield of all salad leaves.
* Young leaves survive slight frost better than mature hearts.
* A mouth-watering range of varieties is available, with many colours, textures and tastes.
* The main pests are slugs, but in dry summers root aphids may kill plants.

Lettuce has a lot going for it. Mild-tasting leaves of intriguing combinations of colour, an ability to grow in relatively cool conditions and stand some frost, and the option for most varieties of producing either a heart or a steady supply of leaves over several months, from one sowing.

June lettuce bed was planted 15 days earlier with (from front): *Canasta*, *Bijou*, and *Jabeque*, netted against rabbits and birds.

The best months for lettuce harvests are April to July, before autumnal mildews become more prevalent. Lettuce leaves in spring and early summer have a refreshing, ultra-healthy crunch and gloss, especially when grown with good compost. They are not bothered by flea beetles, so any holes are from slugs and snails, which definitely are interested in lettuce. Slug numbers are reduced by growing leaf lettuce at wider spacings, and picking regularly, but are more difficult to control under the large, spreading leaves of lettuce hearts.

Think of lettuce plantings in artistic terms, using them to beautify your garden or outdoor space. An appealing range of colour with different lustre and hues will then transfer, on picking, to an attractive, bountiful and regularly filled salad bowl.

Flavour-wise, lettuce is fairly neutral: less powerful than rocket and oriental leaves, less bitter than chicories and endives, less tangy than chards and purslane. So it is fine company in salad with any of these, and especially with small amounts of stronger-tasting herbs such as basil, coriander and dill. I have fun every year experimenting with all the additions and combinations.

NORMAL PATTERN OF GROWTH

Lettuce seed germinates best in slightly warm rather than very warm soil, in spring and autumn better than in hot summer weather. Tiny seedlings grow steadily into plants up to 40cm (16") in height and width, and after three months on average, a heart of paler, crisper leaves will usually develop. This heart solidifies for a week or two before suddenly breaking open and sending out a flowering stem which rises up to 90cm (3") high, carrying tiny pale yellow flowers that eventually transform into tufts of white fluff, with clumps of seeds underneath them. From sowing to seed harvest takes about six months, or ten months from sowings in late summer.

If a heart is not allowed to develop, through continual harvesting of lower leaves, the total harvest is often greater and always more regular from vigorous 'teenage' plants that are not allowed to mature. Rising to flower is delayed, and it happens on a smaller stem.

Not all varieties make firm hearts and there are many different categories of lettuce, all with a range of qualities to their leaves.

SOWING AND SPACING, FOR ALL TYPES

If you sow in rows straight into a bed, I recommend a space of 25-30cm (10-12") between the rows and then thinning plants, when they have about six leaves, to 20cm (8") apart within the row. This allows plenty of room for root development, smaller-leaf lettuce included, allowing the plants a longer life. Also some bare soil between plants makes for fewer slugs, especially if you pick leaves regularly (see opposite as well as pages 21-3, Chapter 2) and remove any weed seedlings before they develop into larger plants. Lettuce can be sown over a long season but three sowings per year should provide leaves every day between May and October at least. Sowing dates are mid-March, late May and mid- to late July. Also, if the first sowing is under cover in January or February, for planting out in March or early April, first leaves can be ready by mid-April. Bring harvests forward by covering plants with fleece, which is best laid on top of them and kept fairly firm rather than flapping in wind.

GROWING

Well-raised lettuce plants resist cold weather. I have had young plants out on nights of -6°C/21°F, frozen under fleece, and they survived and grew well after that. However, hearts do not survive being frozen, see pages 129-31.

Rain is more of a problem than cold, because wet soil is slow to warm and encourages passage of slugs at night. Snails and slugs can be a problem at any time of year, especially if it is continually wet. See Chapter 8, pages 80-82 for ideas on dealing with them.

How your plants grow to maturity will depend on spacing, soil and compost quality, watering and, above all, your harvesting method (see page 129). Weeding is the same as for other crops – do it little and often, keeping the surface weed-free for the morale of both you and your plants.

CONTAINER GROWING

Lettuce grows well in containers, large pots and window boxes. Expect to use about four litres of compost for each lettuce when you want to keep picking leaves for at least two months. See the

Spring lettuce: (from left) *Grenoble Red*, *Bijou* and *Winter Density*, all from home-saved seed, 75 days after sowing.

May lettuce bed before the third harvest.

Before a first harvest in April, 66 days after sowing – see page 134.

cropping examples in Chapter 4, pages 44-6.

I have found that lettuce hearts are a little trickier in containers because slugs always seem to arrive in them sooner or later, unseen at first, and do some deep damage. Be vigilant for slugs, especially just after you have planted seedlings.

WATERING

Since lettuce leaves are at least 90 per cent water and grow quickly, their roots need ready access to moisture. In containers and window boxes, this means watering at least three times a week in sunny, warm weather, or watering every three to five days in larger beds, giving the soil or compost a good soak to at least 15cm (6") depth; this is better than a daily sprinkling, which evaporates more quickly and causes slugs and mildew. Good compost on top of any lettuce bed will help to hold moisture and is one reason why they thrive in it.

As plants grow larger, their needs for water increase and hearting plants are extremely thirsty, suffering tipburn – a rotting of the leaves' extremities – if moisture is insufficient. An advantage of regularly harvesting loose leaves is that this almost never occurs.

PROBLEMS

To reduce slug damage, keep ground clear around lettuce plants, harvest regularly and make the usual slug patrols and checks, as described in Chapter 8. Root aphids are often present and then may become dramatically apparent in

Lollo Rossa in May, after the first harvest of outer leaves.

dry summers especially, when lettuce suddenly falls limp and then dies as its roots are eaten. Consistent watering helps but some late summers can be difficult. Fortunately there are many other salad leaves to grow at that time of year.

Aphids are occasionally abundant on some leaves in early spring. Again watering is a help and they usually diminish as ladybirds and other predators appear.

HARVESTING LEAVES

Picking loose leaves

I recommend picking off any larger, lower leaves by carefully holding the plant with one hand while using the other to gently twist and pull on one leaf at a time. This is more difficult on the first harvest and becomes easier as plants mature over two to three months. On older plants with a firm root system, it's possible to use two hand simultaneously. Stop picking when you have a central rosette of at least six or eight leaves.

This may sound more fiddly and time-consuming than either cutting hearts or cutting across thick rows of young plants. In fact it's the other way round and with a little practice you will find yourself quite quickly gathering a few leaves off many plants, thus composing a pretty collection. Leaves are nearly all healthy and undamaged, as long as you remove the occasional damaged or diseased leaf at every harvest, leaving only healthy ones to grow on.

Compared with picking loose leaves,

cutting a heart is time-consuming when you count all the growing time, then clearing the debris, resowing and so forth. Careful trimming is necessary because of all the mildewed and eaten leaves that always accompany a well-formed lettuce heart.

Also, I nearly always find a slug or two in lettuce hearts, which require careful washing.

Likewise, when leaves are *cut* from quite thickly sown rows of lettuce (and most other salad species), they normally need careful sorting to remove the yellowing and diseased leaves, which have been starved of light and air in the middle and at the bottom of closely growing plants. Further time is lost in waiting for regrowth of the baby central leaves that have been part cut by your knife, and also from having to make extra sowings, because cut plants live less long than carefully picked ones.

So harvest carefully and you will be rewarded! I found the best time to sow in Somerset is late February in the greenhouse, to plant out by the end of March, with a fleece cover over. First harvests are after just one month and we continue picking medium-sized leaves off these same plants, through extremely wet weather and with little slug damage, for up to thirteen weeks. They yield about 28g (1oz) of leaves per plant per week, up to 400g (14oz) per plant.

Picking hearts

Sweetest lettuce leaves are found in their tightly folded hearts, although much leaf colour is lost as leaves turn

Summer lettuce just 18 days after planting, sown 44 days ago.

Steph starts a fifth pick of summer lettuce.

pale. Hearts develop around three months from sowing, depending on the season. Their quality is usually best from June until August, and top weights are achieved in warm, wet seasons. But if it rains and stays damp continually, many outer leaves can be lost to mildew and slugs.

A heart is mature when there is a clear definition of colour between darker outside leaves and those of a paler, tightly folded central rosette. Either slip a knife under the whole plant, and then trim off all damaged leaves until arriving at the good middle ones, or push back the unwanted outer leaves and cut higher up.

If the stump is left undisturbed, with all its leaves removed, some regrowth of baby lettuces often occurs, but harvests are small.

Although lettuce plants are reasonably frost-hardy, the tightly folded leaves of hearts are damaged by freezing, mainly in October when frosts can be of sufficient duration to turn much of a heart to ice, followed by leaves rotting as they thaw.

TYPES OF LETTUCE WITH VARIETAL EXAMPLES

Batavia *Grenoble Red*
Firm, slightly crisp leaves of many colours and shiny hues. Leaves can be picked on a continual basis, leading to plants of notable longevity; otherwise, hearts of pale, crisp leaves will develop. Many varieties are winter-hardy, reflecting their origins in continental or mountainous regions of cold winters.

Butterhead *Marvel of Four Seasons*
Until recently this was the most commonly grown lettuce type in Britain, with soft, pale, waxy leaves enveloping an even paler and waxier heart. Varietal differences include a few with darker and bronze-coloured leaves, while some are winter-hardy, for hearts in the spring. The young leaves of butterhead tend to lie low on the soil, making them hard to harvest as loose leaves, and their popularity has diminished as more people discover the other types of hearting lettuce.

Cos *Lobjoits, Little Gem*
These are lettuces of Greek origin whose growth is healthiest, for the most part, in warm summer weather. Leaves are the darkest green of any lettuce type, with some new reddish hues becoming available, and grow into sweet hearts of variable size. Cos plants are the most upright of all lettuces and therefore lend themselves to easy picking of young leaves. A hybrid variety, *Winter Density*, will stand most winters as a small plant, then makes a sweet heart in spring.

Crisp *Webbs Wonderful, Lakeland*
Dense, pale iceberg hearts are the usual objective when growing these lettuce. Many have been bred for irrigated Californian conditions and to harvest all at the same time, so they heart up evenly and do best in warm summer weather with plenty of sun, yet moist soil around their roots. *Webbs* is an older, less uniform variety with a longer season and tastier leaves, and it is easier to grow.

Loose-leaf *Bijou, Mottistone*
This category includes all lettuce that

do not make firm hearts, having been bred for continual picking or cutting of young leaves. Not waiting for a heart to develop means that harvests start much earlier. The increasing popularity of leaf lettuce means an exciting range of varieties to choose from, of varied colours, shapes and textures.

At the same time, many cos and Batavian lettuces are suitable for harvesting like leaf lettuce. Regular picking of their larger leaves diverts new growth from formation of hearts to production of more outer leaves. Almost every variety of all kinds of lettuce can be picked as though it were officially a loose-leaf type. Those that best lend themselves to this kind of harvesting are recommended below.

A NOTE ON COLOUR

As well as looking strikingly different, dark red lettuces grow differently from green ones:

* They are slower-growing, sometimes at half the rate of green lettuce, making them more susceptible to mildew on older, outer leaves.
* Their flavour is a little bitter.
* They are less appreciated by slugs than green varieties – I often notice untouched red leaves near to slug-holed green lettuce. The deep colour brings an exotic look to the vegetable garden.

VARIETIES OF LETTUCE

Most of these can be treated as loose-leaf and picked regularly; if marked (H) they will also make a firm heart. Unless otherwise indicated, all are suitable for sowing from March to mid-August.

Appleby
Oak-shaped leaves are pale green, compact in shape and pleasantly dense in texture. *Appleby* grows well through most of the season, from sowings between March and July. It is extremely high-yielding and long-lived, but its young leaves are a little tricky to twist off, while later pickings are easier and the payback is longevity of picking, as with *Grenoble Red*.

Bijou
I grow Bijou for its dark red colour alone and it grows well both early and late in the season. Like all the dark red lettuces, it looks wonderful when growing in the salad bed. It offers fewer leaves than green varieties, flowers earlier and has a slightly bitter flavour.

Cantarix
Vigorous growth of medium-sized red oak leaves. *Cantarix* makes a compact, attractive plant and produces decent tasting leaves for 10-13 weeks.

Chartwell and Claremont (H)
The best cos-leaf varieties I am aware of, with dark green leaves of compact shape, good flavour, easy to pick and reliable in any season. Can be allowed to grow into hearts of good flavour.

Freckles
An excellent cos variety that grows well in most conditions, and can be high-yielding. The freckling varies from plant to plant – some leaves are covered in maroon spots and some are mostly pale green. But all leaves are thin, tender and sadly a favourite of slugs!

Grenoble Red (H)
A remarkable variety for consistent growth in spring and autumn espe-

Picking outer leaves of Winter Density for the seventh week.

cially; also it boasts resistance to mildew and slugs. Compact, bronzed leaves are a little tricky to pick off young plants, but this is compensated by plentiful, easier pickings as plants mature. Sow late August to early September for overwintering outdoors, it has excellent frost-resistance. Hearting can lead to tipburn should moisture run short.

Little Gem (H)

One of the quicker-maturing varieties with first hearts by early June from a March sowing. They are deliciously sweet and slightly waxy, but a lot of slug-eaten and diseased outer leaves usually need trimming off, especially after midsummer when mildew invades. It can be picked as a leaf lettuce. Last sowings by late July should be spaced closer at 20x20cm (8x8") because the last sowings grow a little smaller in early autumn's darker days.

The popularity of *Little Gem* has resulted in some nice variants. *Maureen* is a *Little Gem* type of good vigour, longevity and flavour. *Amaze* is a *Little Gem* with spaces of dark red on its outer leaves.

Lobjoits (H)

It is possible to harvest large, rather loose and pleasantly sweet hearts weighing over 1kg (2lb), especially in a wet summer, as *Lobjoits* requires plenty of water to heart up well. If too dry, the outsides of its leaves will rot, sometimes right into the heart.

Lollo Rossa Tuska

Lollo Rossa varieties give fluffy and pretty leaves, though of average flavour. The variety *Tuska* is notable for being more pink than deep red, and for giving harvests for an exceptional number of

The same lettuces after a first harvest of 7.14kg (15lb 11oz) leaves from 120 plants – see page 127.

weeks – up to 15 in spring and early summer. The first pick is low to the ground, then becomes reasonably easy. Its leaves look gorgeous when backlit by early or late sunshine.

Maravilla de Verano (also called Canasta) (H)

A fine summer lettuce, whose leaves are firm, shiny and mostly pale green with bronzing at the edges. It works well as a leaf lettuce or makes a characteristically pale, crisp Batavian heart. Outer and heart leaves have good flavour. Best sown in April for cropping late spring to early summer; it is prone to root aphids in late summer.

Mottistone

Quite a small cos with round, Batavian-style leaves, all beautifully mottled and bronzed. They are held close to the stem so the first few need careful picking; thereafter a steady number of leaves can be picked for up to three months as it is slow to flower.

Red Sails

Extremely fast-growing with crinkly bronze leaves – grows especially well in cooler spring weather. *Red Sails* needs frequent picking unless you want really large leaves.

Rosemoor (H)

Red leaves of a deep hue are quite long and easy to pick, of fair flavour and grow vigorously. *Rosemoor* crops for a longer season than many other red varieties and looks great in both garden and salads.

OTHER LOOSE-LEAF VARIETIES

Aruba
Dark red, long and thin oak leaves.

Catalogna
Vigorous, bright green and long leaves of unremarkable flavour.

Mascara
Bright red oak-leaf type.

Red Fire
High-yielding frilly, bronzed leaves of average flavour.

Rubens Red (H)
A hearting cos with tasty bronze leaves, good for regular picking as loose leaves.

Salad Bowl (Red and Green)
Thin, fragile oak leaves, prone to mildew.

Solstice
Large, frilled, bright green leaves, fast-growing and good for spring harvests.

OTHER HEARTING VARIETIES

The following varieties should be sown from March to July and spaced at 25x25cm (10x10"), unless otherwise mentioned.

Butterhead

Buttercrunch
Fast-maturing, extra waxy, pale hearts.

Marvel of Four Seasons
Hardy and with an attractive rosy edge to its leaves. Sow from March to September.

May Queen
Old-fashioned overwintering lettuce. Sow early September to heart in May.

Roxy
A red butterhead, darker colour than *Marvel of Four Seasons* and smaller. Space at 20x20cm (8x8").

Crisp

Ice Queen
On the small side with shiny, remarkably pointed and crunchy leaves.

Saladin
Standard iceberg. Sow April to June, space at 30x30cm (12x12").

Webbs Wonderful
Easier to grow than *Saladin* with a smaller, tastier and more textured heart.

LETTUCE MIXTURES

Seed companies offer packets of mixed lettuce seed, a simple way to grow a variety of leaves. However, you are slightly at their mercy in terms of the mix of ingredients, which may not contain your favourites, and the differing patterns of growth make harvesting uneven.

Because lettuce seed keeps so well, for up to five years, it may be more fun and practical to create your own mix of a few favoured varieties.

CHAPTER TWELVE

ENDIVES AND CHICORIES

A RANGE OF BEAUTIFUL, BITTERSWEET LEAVES

Brief summary

* Strong-flavoured leaves are firm-textured and slightly bitter.
* Hearts are of sweeter flavour and often quite large.
* Sow from May to mid-August for loose leaves.
* Plants for hearting are best sown after the longest day, from 21 June until late July for chicories, and until early August for endives.
* These salad plants are ideal second crops, to follow early vegetables such as broad beans, peas and even onions.
* Endives have either long leaves with curly leaflets (frizzy) or smooth, broader leaves (scarole). Both have the potential to make hearts.
* Chicory leaves have an enormous range of shapes and colours, and many can be picked as loose leaves. The main hearting types are pale green sugarloaf and vivid red and white radicchios.
* Plants survive frost better than lettuce but hearting plants are vulnerable to moderate frost.
* In mild winters, some plants from early autumn sowings can survive and make hearts in April.
* Slugs can damage leaves, especially of young plants. Rabbits love baby endives.

Late autumn: (from front) endive, oriental leaves and rocket after seven weeks of harvests.

These leaves, descended from blue flowering wild chicory, deserve to be grown more than they are, in Britain at least. Their trademarks are a wide range of colours and flavours, often intriguingly bitter-sweet, and an ability to thrive in the dark days of late autumn and winter.

While being members, like lettuce, of the Compositae plant family, endives and chicories are different in two important ways. Firstly, as well as being more bitter, their leaves are higher in dry matter, so they offer plenty to chew on, and store well after picking. Secondly, they need sowing later in the year, because the lengthening days of spring encourage them to flower, while the shortening days of autumn lead to plenty of leafy growth and also to sub-

stantial hearts when they have been sown in high summer. These are useful assets when balanced against lettuce's relatively lower-quality growth and more watery flavour in late season.

Growing these exciting hearts is not difficult. By growing hearts as well as leaves, you can enjoy great contrasts of flavour and colour. Northern Italians eat chicory hearts hot, looking on them as we do cabbage. Their more bitter flavour takes getting used to, but they are less prone to pests than cabbage and make a beautiful feature in the autumn garden.

A further possibility is to grow special varieties of chicory for forcing. Their roots are dug up in autumn and brought indoors to a dark, warmer place to force pale, bittersweet chicons.

29 June: endives and brassicas in the seed tray (to prick out) were sown just three days earlier.

NORMAL PATTERN OF GROWTH

Early growth is a little slower than lettuce, as leaves are slightly tougher and contain less water. From sowings in spring, plants will remain rather small before flowering, depending on the variety. For example, any chicory hearts that do form in early summer, although sometimes looking promising for a while, will suddenly break open and transform into a flower stem.

Late summer and early autumn growth is more predictable and hearts can become quite large – up to 2kg (4lb 6oz) for sugarloaf chicory. This is a great help in mitigating the leaves' bitterness and introduces some pleasantly sweet flavour.

Hearts of endives remain half open, less dense than lettuce but with proportionately more small leaves that are pale and attractive. In the damp, cooler weather of autumn, they often start to rot at the edges soon after maturing; frizzy endives in particular need eating as soon as their hearts mature.

Chicory hearts last better and can also be cut and stored indoors. Once tightly folded they are at some risk – depending on variety – from the same browning at the edges as endives, though it is less visible. Decaying leaves can be peeled away and sometimes a fine small heart may be found inside an outer sheath of brown, rotten leaves.

SOWING

Since most early growth is happening in warmer, drier months of the year, seedlings are easier to bring on than those of early lettuce. I still recommend use of indoor facilities if you have them, because slugs are more than partial to baby leaves and small plants of endive and chicory.

First sowings are best in June, for example to make chicory hearts by late August. A few varieties for leaves, such as *Bianca Riccia da Taglio* endive and *Treviso Svelta* chicory, are suitable for sowing as early as late April but will grow larger and for longer if sown after early June.

Some hearting endives will make a head in August from sowings in late May, check the varieties section on pages 145-7 to see which ones are best for this. Otherwise, June 21 is a top sowing date for fine autumn hearts, and any sowings through July, even into early August, should have time to make a reasonable cluster of blanched leaves. In mild autumns, hearts can be enjoyed through November from sowings made in early August.

For chicory hearts, early to mid-July is the best time, as sowings in the last third of July can sometimes run out of growing time before hearts of any size can develop.

SPACING

Spacing for production of loose leaves is similar to lettuce – no more than 25x 25cm (10x10") for individual plants, to give regular pickings of larger leaves and long-lived plants. Try closer spacings as little as 2cm apart in rows 20cm apart (1x8") if you want to keep cutting small leaves.

July: these endive were pricked into modules 13 days ago.

Sowings of suitable endive varieties in late June and July have sufficient time, in well-composted and moist soil, to make large hearts, so a spacing of 30x30cm (12x12") is the minimum if you want them to keep growing. After mid-September and into October their hearts grow paler and denser, potentially heavy and a great treat for early autumn meals.

Most chicories for hearting are potentially large plants and long-lived, so a spacing of 30x30cm (12x12") is advisable, even a little more for the sugarloaves.

GROWING

Once plants are established, growth is rapid in their main season of late summer warmth. Watering is worth-while in dry weather. In damp summers, be wary of slugs when seedlings are small; night patrols in early August are often worthwhile.

As endives and chicories become large and established, they tolerate some nibbling by slugs of their older, outer leaves which often afford moist shelter to slugs and snails. At this stage it is worthwhile having a look underneath and picking off any molluscs you find off the undersides of the leaves, to stop them grazing on other small plants nearby.

Regularly picked, leaf chicory from an early June sowing should last the whole season and even into the following spring. Spacing can be in a row 30cm (12") from other plants, with chicories at 5-7cm (2-3") apart, which gives space for them to grow healthy leaves

These chicories were planted five days earlier, and netted against rabbits.

and even some mini-hearts if you leave them alone.

CONTAINER GROWING

Leaf endive and chicory are more worthwhile in containers than hearts, which tend to fill up with slugs and become difficult to water adequately when nearing maturity; this is because they need so much water and their large leaves tend to deflect it.

Plant any varieties recommended for leaf production (see below) and harvest some every few days to lessen slug problems, make watering easier and give you regular harvests. As for lettuce, about four litres of compost per plant should provide the resources to keep them cropping.

WATERING

These fast-growing autumn salads may run short of water at a time when soil is often dry, especially when they are following an earlier vegetable crop. Moisten soil before planting and, unless it is a wet season, be generous once plants are growing vigorously in early autumn.

PROBLEMS

Slugs are fond of tender young seedlings but later growth seems of less interest, so hearts are often mostly clean. Success is more likely from raising plants in plugs or modules, rather than sowing direct. Also this gives more time for preceding vegetables or

Chicory *Variegata da Lusia.*

Harvesting an endive – this is the most I would remove at a time.

salad crops to finish, as all chicories and endives make an excellent second crop of vegetables.

Rabbits seem to like endives more than any other salad, and they are not easy to fence out, it's best to use bird netting over transplants (see p.141).

Both endive and radicchio hearts are prone to rot at their leaf margins once fully mature; some experience is needed to learn the best moments for harvesting. Although frost may damage hearts, I find they mostly survive down to about -4°C (23°F) and colder if hearts are still loose. If a -5°C (23°F) or harder frost is forecast, I recommend harvesting all firm hearts, then keeping them in a polythene bag until required, at about 5°C (40°F) if possible; they should keep for a month or more.

REMOVING OLD ROOTS

By May, any remaining chicory roots will be starting to flower. I cut around them with a trowel and pull out the central rootball, including its largest feeder roots, then spread some compost and plant beans or courgettes, or sow beetroot, etc.

HARVESTING LEAVES

Loose leaves

It is not always easy to pick individual endive leaves because they tend to cluster together, lying quite close to the soil. But a pretty yellow variety called *Bianca Riccia da Taglio* has a more open habit of growth and longer, more accessible leaves, as does the green *Romanesca da Taglio*.

Normally we pick outer leaves of endive *Frenzy*, but in November regrowth is small so this is a final cut.

Some endives lend themselves to careful cutting just above their crown, about 2-3cm (1") above the soil surface. I have found *Frenzy* and *Louviers* best, offering several harvests off the same root, starting in early summer. The most straightforward leaf chicory is *Treviso Svelta*, with long, matt, oval-shaped leaves that are green with red spots, turning dark red in colder weather. Plants can be cut frequently, with just a few leaves, or left longer to make a loose heart.

Hearts

Hearts vary – check the varietal descriptions to see what you should expect. Endive hearts are loose and open; chicory hearts are mostly tightly folded.

Because they are all somewhat different and do not always stand well before starting to rot – depending on the weather and exact time of year – they may not always be at their peak just when you want them, but should be close to matching your requirements as long as you respect the sowing dates.

Some slug-eaten, rotting, yellowing and somewhat bitter outer leaves will need discarding when plants are cut, but there should also be a large number of pristine, beautiful, tender, brightly coloured and sweeter leaves in the plants' centres.

TYPES OF ENDIVE WITH VARIETAL EXAMPLES

Hearting frizzy (*frisée*) *Frenzy, Aery*
Frizzy, or *frisée,* describes any endives with deeply serrated leaves. Leaves are mostly long and thin with either flat or curly 'teeth' along their length. Leaf colour ranges from dark green to pale yellow. Best season for hearting is September and October if it is not too cold; any plants maturing after that will be smaller and at risk of rotting from damp or in the event of significant frost.

Hearting scarole *Natacha*
Scarole broad-leaved endives are usually grown for hearting; often of a rather pale green colour, they have much rounder and fleshier leaves than frizzy endives. Their hearts can mature to a considerable size in September and are less fragile than those of frizzy endives, but you still need to watch carefully for the leaves turning brown.

Palla Rossa radicchio chicory in September, three months after sowing.

Leaf endive *Bianca Riccia da Taglio*
Some endives can be regularly picked or cut and keep producing leaves over a long period. This works well from sowings as early as May.

VARIETIES OF LEAF AND HEARTING ENDIVES

Varieties mentioned here are ones I have grown, but there are many more and I urge you to experiment with others you may come across, on foreign holidays or as they become available here. British seed companies are beginning to offer a sample of the wide range available in mainland Europe.

Natacha is my reference variety here and carries a detailed description which is mostly applicable to the other varieties, except for the differences I mention. The ability to make a blanched heart is marked (H).

Bianca Riccia da Taglio
Leaf frizzy. I like this variety for its luminous pale yellow colour, the relative ease of picking its long-stemmed leaves and their mild flavour. First sowings in April will crop for a month or so before flowering and add variety to the predominantly lettuce salads of spring. Sowings from May to July will crop for longer and with higher yields. Usually I twist off the larger leaves around its base but cutting is also possible, about 2-3cm (1") above the crown, and harvestable regrowth happens within two to three weeks. For this to happen, make sure the knife slices through leaves above the firm stem so that, from

one horizontal cut, they will all separate without needing a further cut to part them. Leaves have attractive pink colouration on their lower stem.

Cornet de Bordeaux (H)

Hearting scarole. Similar to *Bubikopf* below, except that its heart leaves are longer and more pointed, and sometimes cluster into a cone of yellow leaves.

Fine Maraichere (H)

Hearting frizzy. Larger- and darker-leaved than *Frenzy* – longer, heavier, glossier and with substantial curly edges. Sow after about mid-June for well-filled hearts; last sowings by early August will mature in October and November, when there is some risk of rotting and of frost damage to the more tender hearting leaves. A covering of fleece can save the day if it is unusually cold.

Frenzy (H)

Leaf or hearting frizzy. A heart of pale and finely desiccated leaves can be obtained when *Frenzy* is allowed to grow for eight to ten weeks after sowings made from June to mid-August.

Alternatively, from a sowing in May, leaves can be harvested many times off the same root between late June and September. As plants of *Frenzy* mature, their leaves become thinner and more numerous, and cutting them every fortnight or three weeks gives a plentiful supply. Use a sharp knife, horizontally, about 1-2cm (½-1") above the plant's base. A few yellowing outer leaves will need discarding, especially after longer intervals between harvests. If spaced at 30x30cm (12x12") the roots have plenty of nutrients and water to tap into, resulting in steady growth over a long period

Three varieties of endive: (from front) *Aery, Bianca Riccia da Taglio, Frenzy.*

until at least mid-October, depending on the weather.

Natacha (H)

A large plant with a well-filled, reasonably blanched heart. Best sowing dates are through July until mid-August for maturity after mid-September, when mild temperatures and a balance of sun and rain are just what endives like. But cold nights and extreme wet can cause rotting so keep an eye on them, especially leaf margins, which are the first to show faint brownness; this can quickly lead to many leaves rotting.

Young plants are more frost-hardy than hearted ones, so a late-September sowing may survive until the following spring and make a small heart before flowering. Watch it closely, as the flowering stem in April can quickly rob a decent heart of its best leaves. Alternatively, a few outer leaves at a time can be picked off through late winter and early spring, to provide a continual supply of smaller, more bitter but healthily green leaves.

Pancalieri

Vigorous, large, dark green leaves can be picked regularly; the plant will heart up nicely too. Sow from early June to early August.

Riccia Romanesca da Taglio (also called Romanesco)

Leaf frizzy. More bitter than all of the above with large, dark green leaves that hang loose and never cluster. Regular picking works best, before any yellowing of older leaves. They grow well in cool weather but dislike moderate frost. Plants may survive the winter to regrow for a while in early spring. New sowings in spring tend to flower before many leaves are produced.

TYPES OF CHICORY WITH VARIETAL EXAMPLES

Sugarloaf hearts *Pain de Sucre*
Large, usually tall and thin, pale green plants with folded leaves which tighten up from about September onwards. Hearts have creamy-coloured leaves, thin and papery at the edge, crunchier towards the centre. They stand frost down to about -3°C (27°F) or -4°C (25°F), but if lower temperatures are forecast, cut hearts that are mature and store in a cool place for up to six weeks.

Radicchio hearts *Palla Rossa*
Some of the most beautiful salad leaves occur in radicchio hearts; crisp and firm leaves which are mottled or streaked in various combinations of red, white and pale green. *Palla Rossa* plants have round, red hearts of more or less tightly wrapped leaves and are usually named after their place of origin in Italy, such as Lusia or Verona. The standard *Palla Rossa* variety comes from Chioggia and is less esteemed, flavour- and texture-wise, by Italian cooks. *Treviso* radicchios have longer, thinner, more succulent and sometimes waxy leaves of intense colour. They grow more slowly, so are correspondingly highly priced and sought after. Their hearts are really a collection of smaller leaves without any tight binding – but see 'Forcing chicories' on page 149.

Leaf chicory *Treviso Svelta*
Many varieties are suitable for picking or cutting at regular intervals. Chicory regrows better after cutting than most endive and lettuce, but harvesting loose leaves rather than hearts means that they are more bitter. Leaves come in

Palla Rossa chicory – this plant's heart will fill some more.

various shades of red and green and have many different shapes.

Forcing chicories *Witloof*

Varieties of chicory bred for forcing make large roots which are best trimmed of all leaves and dug up between November and Christmas; they then need keeping in total darkness so that they grow chicons of yellow leaves. Any light will cause these chicons to open a little and become slightly bitter and green, instead of sweet and yellow. See pages 150-3 for information on varieties to use, how to grow the chicons and the best temperatures for bringing them on.

VARIETIES OF HEARTING CHICORY

Bianca di Milano

A compact sugarloaf. The sowing date is important if you want well blanched leaves in a firm, heavy heart, papery at its edge and crisp in the middle; aim for the week between 28 June and 5 July. Later sowings until about July 15th grow well but fold into smaller, looser hearts. These, however, will stand frost better than the large, tight ones, which also risk rotting at their edges, although these leaves can be peeled off to reveal a dense, white heart. Plants with loose hearts can stand through winter for harvesting as late as March.

Grumolo Verde

Small green heart or leaf. This variety is best suited to sowing in late July or early August for standing the winter as fair-sized but loose-leaved plants, to make small and thoroughly welcome hearts in March and April. There can also be some tasty regrowth after cutting this heart. *Grumolo Rosso* grows a little smaller and with attractive red colouration. *Grumolo Bionda* is less frost-hardy and seems more inclined to heart up before winter if leaves are not picked.

Palla Rossa

Red radicchio. I warmly recommend the selection made by Bingenheim Saatgut. The heads of their *Palla Rossa* stand for weeks longer than others I have grown, from sowings as early as 10 June. Sow until 20 July for hearts as late as November, and to the year's end if frost holds off. Plants mature at different rates from one sowing and have slightly looser, less regular heads than F1 varieties of *Palla Rossa*.

Palla Rossa di Verona

Exemplifies the difficulties I have had in finding out how to grow hearting radicchios, because mine never look like the ones in seed packet photos!

Palla Rossa Marzatica

A little frost-hardy, this is one of the best varieties for late red hearts, though extremely variable – some plants are just long leaves. Sow late July for Christmas radicchio.

Puntarelle di Galatina

This is a most unusual chicory and fun to grow! Sow in late June or the first half of July and watch it grow into a huge green plant with leaves like a dandelion. By October some plants will send up hollow shoots of 'asparagus chicory', keep cutting the shoots for repeated harvests, even into spring if winter leaves the root intact.

Rossa di Treviso

Makes small clusters of pointed, dark red leaves in open ground in late autumn, turning almost black in frosty weather. They are striking and tasty. For extra value, try digging up the roots and forcing some small chicons, usually one per root (see below)

Sugarloaf, Pan di Zucchero

Tall sugarloaf. Similar to *Milano* above but longer and heavier with slightly thinner leaves. It can weigh up to 2kg when all goes well.

Variegata di Castelfranco

This is an enigma, offering a loose head in late autumn of prettily speckled leaves that mostly resist frost and sometimes transform into a small heart in late winter or early spring, although I find that some plants' leaves just rot around their edges. *Castelfranco*'s roots can also be dug before Christmas to force, see below.

Variegata di Lusia

Only Franchi Seeds (see Resources) offer this variety and it has changed since I first grew it, from a compact hearting plant of bright pink and yellow leaves, to a taller chicory with paler hearts which are more attractive to slugs, best harvested by November.

VARIETAL EXAMPLES OF LEAF CHICORY

Catalogna Gigante da Chioggia

A most vigorous plant with welcome larger leaves when many plants are growing less strongly. Its thick pale stems can be surprisingly sweet when a little blanched by other stems outside them and the long, fleshy, serrated leaves are of agreeable flavour, although a little prone to browning at their edges.

Red-ribbed Dandelion

This is really a leaf chicory and should be treated as such; best sown from May until mid-August. Leaves are best picked or cut at least weekly, unless you like them really long and with thick stems. Clean old leaves away in December and look for new ones in March and April; if left beyond that, there will grow a long and straggly stem with pretty pale blue flowers.

Treviso Svelta

An excellent variety for many harvests of prettily coloured leaves, more green in summer and red in cold weather. It can be picked or cut in many ways – remove small leaves as you need them or allow plants to grow about 25cm (10") high with small pink leaves at their semi-hearting centres. Any unpicked larger leaves die back in late autumn but roots should survive and make new leaves in early spring before flowering in May.

GROWING CHICORIES FOR FORCING

First of all, grow chicories through the summer and autumn. Sometimes these offer a small tasty heart but most leaves are large and bitter, and are trimmed off when the chicory roots are dug out. These roots are then brought indoors where, in darkness and some warmth, they grow numbers of chicons of variable size and from two to twelve or so off each root.

Picking *Palla Rossa Romea* of outer leaves rather than allowing a heart.

SOWING

Sow between early May and mid-June, depending on how large you want the roots. Slugs love the seedlings, so it is best sow two seeds per module in the greenhouse, thin to one and plant at 30x30cm (12x12") in late June or early July, often after early beans and potatoes, or between onions.

GROWING

Once established, these chicories are robust and vigorous until November, when their outer leaves start to die back, leaving a cluster of semi-hearted leaves that can be eaten, although they tend to rot quite quickly.

HARVESTING ROOTS

Roots are ready to harvest from this point and want digging out carefully, as any branch roots that are left behind will grow like weeds the following year. Trim off all leaves, right down to the white tops of the roots.

GROWING CHICONS

Location and temperature are important; choose from these two options when growing chicons:

1) Place in buckets or large pots so that the top 3cm (1") of roots is above the level of compost packed around the lower part of the roots. Roots can be packed in together – say, three to a

Treviso chicory in November.

25cm (10") pot, depending on how large they have grown. They are best grown in a dark cupboard or shed to keep chicons firm.

2) Place two or three roots in a polythene sack or bin-liner to conserve moisture and exclude light. Roots can be laid out horizontally; chicons will grow upwards and at right angles to them.

The first method gives roots a longer life with second and perhaps third re-growths, but these later pickings are sometimes of lower quality, so the simpler second option is worthwhile and can produce some fine chicons. Nearly all of the main first crop of chicons is coming out of the root, rather than being fed from compost in a pot.

Chicons are almost the only salad whose speed of growth is controlled by the gardener. Place roots in a warm airing cupboard and chicons will appear quickly, growing to full size in two to four weeks. Alternatively, keep them at 'cellar temperature' of about 11°C (52°F) for harvests after eight to twelve weeks.

HARVESTING CHICONS

Chicons show maturity by losing a little quality on their outer leaves and then by elongating as a flowering stalk is initiated. Harvest any like that and thin out small chicons where a lot have appeared. The harvesting period depends on temperature: fast growth may result in one large harvest, slow growth in several smaller ones.

Final harvests are in April and roots can then be composted.

VARIETIES OF FORCING CHICONS

Palla Rossa di Treviso

In their region of origin, these chicories are dug out from early November, pruned of all leaves and straggly roots, then placed in troughs of top-quality water of a mild temperature in large barns or hangars. Within three weeks or so they have grown beautiful clusters of pink, top-flavoured leaves which look like flowers and are of exquisite flavour. We cannot replicate this in the UK, but reasonable and pretty chicons will grow from roots placed in compost or bags and kept dark, preferably at a temperature of 12-18°C (54-65°F).

Witloof

The standard, reliable variety.

Zoom F1

Extra vigour and yellow colour.

CHAPTER THIRTEEN

LEAVES OF THE CABBAGE FAMILY

ORIENTAL LEAVES, KALES, ROCKETS AND OTHERS

Brief summary

* The main period of sowing is late June to early September; best results from sowings in August.

* Check the varied dates for each different type of plant.

* Most of the pests that love brassicas are less numerous after late summer.

* The main period of outdoor harvest is mid-August to November.

* Light frost is tolerated and a few of these plants survive extreme winters.

* Without protection, leaf harvests from December to early March are usually small.

* Apart from Chinese cabbage, these plants make leaves, not hearts.

* There is a huge variety of leaf flavours, sizes and colours

* Growth is rapid so watering is necessary, especially when late summer and early autumn are dry.

* These are ideal second crops in the garden after peas, beans, carrots, lettuce, etc.

Autumn salad leaves: (from front) mustards, rocket, chicories, and Chinese cabbage under mesh.

Plants of the cabbage family are programmed to set seed when days are lengthening up to midsummer, so avoid sowing them in spring if you want leaves rather than flowers. Also, all members of the cabbage family are highly attractive to many kinds of pest, especially in spring and summer.

Brassica's virtues include rapid growth from sowings in late summer, a greater ability to survive light frosts and make new leaves in winter than most other salads, and a wide range of spicy flavours and leaf shapes, often with attractive colours as well. Should you have an indoor growing space, their cool-season capabilities can be exploited more fully to enjoy significant winter harvests (see Chapter 19).

PATTERN OF GROWTH

Having originated in oceanic, temperate climates, brassicas tolerate normal winter conditions in countries such as Britain, Ireland and Japan, as well as the coastal regions of north-west Europe, but struggle in dry weather and severe continental frost. During winter there is little new growth but before flowering in late winter and early spring, there is a short period when leaves grow and renew, especially if it has been a mild winter. This is a source of valuable salads in March and April, at a time when many gardens are bare of fresh green vegetables to harvest.

As days lengthen in spring they develop a flower stem, often long, thin and edible when young, with bright

A box of mustards, 42 days after a September sowing.

August brassica sowings at different stages with turnips and spinach just emerging.

yellow and tasty flowers that open fast in any spring warmth. Some brassicas, such as cauliflowers and broccoli, have been bred to grow larger flower buds, which we eat before they open out.

SOWING

Seed of most brassicas germinates fast, with the first green shoots visible within four days in summer. July sowings are more likely to encounter flea beetles, September sowings may suffer slug damage as they grow more slowly.

Different speeds of growth and leaf qualities make for different best sowing dates – see the descriptions below.

All can be raised in modules or small pots, or sown direct; and they grow well as clumps, so you can multi-sow two to four seeds per module. You will find most success with sowing under cover, to restrict pest damage.

SPACING

For direct sowing use row widths of 30cm (12") and thin plants to 2-8cm (1-3"), depending on whether you want baby or medium-sized leaves.

Plant multi-sown modules at 22x22cm (9x9") for clumps of medium sized leaves.

GROWING

Rapid growth means high demands for moisture and in all except the wettest summers, some watering improves the quality of growth. Autumn is easier in this respect, offering warmth and moisture in fair proportions.

Composted soil holds moisture well, and the beds featured in Chapter 3 are eminently suitable for brassica leaves, as are window boxes or pots filled with nutritious compost and watered regularly.

Growth slows in October, after which new leaves are small and precious until faster growth in March, depending on weather conditions. A cloche covering through winter can double the harvest at least, and a cover of fleece will increase it, though less effectively.

CONTAINER GROWING

All of these plants, grown for frequent picking, are ideal to grow in containers, particularly since they slot into a 'container rotation' as second crops. You could, for example, grow lettuce from April to July, then mustards and kale from August; or spinach from April, followed by lettuce from June, then rocket and mizuna from September. See also 'Salad rotation' in Chapter 2, pages 24-7.

WATERING

Rapid growth means regular watering in dry weather – say, twice a week – and a good soaking when plants are larger. Containers need water even in damp weather, often into the autumn, but very little in winter.

Mesh is removed from pak choi, kale, and kohlrabi in September, just 19 days after planting.

Chinese cabbage *Yuki* and *Scarvita F1*, just planted in August.

The same Chinese cabbage 12 days later – it grows fast!

Many kale varieties in early autumn, 58 days after sowing.

PROBLEMS

Quality of leaves in summer is improved by protecting with fine mesh to keep insects at bay, although a few flea beetles still find their way in.

Caterpillars can cause significant damage, most notably to Chinese cabbage and pak choi in late summer and early autumn. If there are any holes in fleece or mesh, damage can be worse than on unprotected plants, because of less access to predators.

I summer I spray brassica leaves with *Bacillus thuringiensis*, (commonly known as Bt) which is made of soil bacteria. It makes them undigestible to caterpillars, but even so there is some damage to hearts of Chinese cabbage, the most difficult vegetable.

Slugs are a continual problem, with Chinese cabbage, pak choi and komatsuna their most sought-after victims.

Larger leaves in autumn suffer some brown rings of fungal decay. It is best to remove all damaged leaves and keep picking small, healthier regrowth.

Sometimes plants wilt for no obvious reason, usually because the maggots of cabbage root fly are eating their roots. Fleece and mesh help to keep them out but damage is mainly confined to weaker plants.

Grey and white aphids are sometimes invasive on kale in winter and spring, mainly when there is little frost. Adding compost to enrich the soil is the best preventative remedy, and spraying with water reduces their numbers.

HARVESTING

Leaves

The choice is between cutting and picking. Cutting works best in warm weather when regrowth is rapid. Any decapitation of baby leaves close to plants' growing points means they take longer to regrow; this is most apparent in cold conditions. Cutting is quick for hundreds of micro or baby leaves, but is a one-off harvest when the stem is cut through.

For a longer period of picking through winter months, I recommend looking after plants by pinching, twisting or cutting individual leaves as they mature. 'Mature' means before they start to lose quality and develop fungal damage or slug holes. This applies to quite small leaves in winter much larger ones in autumn and spring, so watch plants and maintain them on top form through good harvesting.

Oriental leaves are often shallow-rooted and you must take care while picking leaves not to disturb the fragile roots. Long thumbnails are useful for pinching through stems; or you can cut leaves singly.

Have a discards bucket for any old, discoloured and eaten leaves, to make subsequent harvests easier, and to reduce hiding-places for slugs.

Hearts

Red and white cabbage are often used in winter salads, while here we are looking at the pale, crisp hearts of Chinese cabbage. As hearts form, their outer leaves quickly decay. It is best to harvest at this stage, trim off damaged leaves and store in cool moisture – say, in a polythene bag in the fridge, where they will keep for at least a month.

GENERIC / VARIETAL DESCRIPTIONS

Most of the headings in this section are species of plants. Because they are all slightly different vegetables, I include some specific sowing and harvest dates for each. The varieties I mention are generally available and have grown well for me.

Oriental vegetables

Salad vegetables from the orient are mostly of the huge cabbage family. Their leaves are often faster-growing and more tender than others considered here, but with no less flavour, and spicy mustard tastes are one of their characteristics.

Chinese broccoli/kale (also called Kailaan)

Sow: August
Space: 25x25cm (10x10")
Harvest: Late August to October
The smooth and slightly waxy leaves resist flea beetle better than most others considered here. It grows fast, becoming quite large as small flower buds also appear. All parts of the plant are good to eat and extremely tasty – leaves, stems and flowers, although if you keep eating the leaves, there will certainly be less broccoli! The leaves are slightly firm and shiny, closer to European cabbage leaves than many oriental brassicas.

Chinese cabbage

Varieties: *Kaboko F1* for small and rapid-growing hearts, *Blues F1* for larger hearts, *Scarvita F1* for crimson/pink hearts.
Sow: Mid-July to mid-August
Space: 30x30cm (12x12")
Harvest: September to November
The favourite meal of many garden pests. When I grew a couple in a bed of salad plants alongside 20 other different vegetables, it was the only one to suffer appreciable damage from slugs, which seem drawn to Chinese cabbage from far and wide. One of the plants somehow made a heart but its outer leaves contained slimy monsters. Caterpillars are the other chief pest.

Komatsuna (also called Japanese mustard spinach)

Sow: Late July to early September
Space: variable
Harvest: late August to October
Komatsuna grows rapidly to large leaves that are good in stir-fries. *Red Komatsuna* offers smaller leaves of a deep crimson hue, less attractive to slugs. My preferred timing is to sow a few seeds in late August for leaves from late September and through October, when they grow more slowly. Watch out for slugs.

Chinese cabbage *Scarvita F1*.

Outdoor land cress in February, netted against pigeons.

Leaf radish

Varieties: *Sai Sai* (green) and *Red Stemmed*
Sow: July to September
Space: 15x15cm (6x6") or 30x8cm (12x3")
Harvest: August to October
Mild leaves grow abundantly on these fine plants, bred to be smooth and without the hairs normally found on radish leaves. Large seeds are easy to sow and fast to grow. Leaves grow large and darker if left unpicked, and more fibrous. I prefer to pick medium-sized leaves frequently rather than cut all of them.

The radish root is thin and white (rose-coloured for the red-stemmed variety), edible but not especially tender, and is vulnerable to attack by cabbage root fly, so two or three sowings up to mid-September should ensure leaves from midsummer to late autumn. Some plants survive frost but winter harvests are small, before improving briefly in early spring.

Mibuna

Sow: Late July to September
Space: 20x5cm (8x2")
Harvest: August to November
Mibuna grows like mizuna but has different leaves – dark green, smooth-edged, long and thin. They are best eaten small, so cutting plants at close spacings works well. By mid-October many leaves are often blotchy with brown fungi, but mibuna survives average British winters fairly well, making new leaves from late winter into April and some tasty flowering shoots as well.

Mitsuba (also called Japanese parsley)

Sow: June to early August
Space: 25cm x 25cm (10" x 10")
Harvest: July onwards.
Not a brassica but related to carrots and parsley, of the Umbelliferae family. Germination and growth is slow and late spring sowings may flower before making many leaves, but cutting their stem should encourage new leaves. Mitsuba is a hardy perennial and withstands frost, but prefers protection from an average British winter (see Chapter 19), and likes some shade plus moisture in summer.

Mizuna

Varieties: Often unspecified; *Waido* has fatter stems and more compact leaves
Sow: Late July to September
Space: 20-25cmx5-10cm (8-10"x2-4") – many spacings work, for different-sized leaves
Harvest: August onwards.
Of rapid growth with juicy, mild-flavoured leaves, especially when young. July sowings are usually more holed by flea beetle and rise to flower more quickly than later sowings. Mizuna is good for cutting about 2.5cm (1") above ground level. If you thin seedlings out to about 20cm (8") apart in each row, the remaining plants will grow large with long white stems. Harvest them by cutting across and above their base, removing all damaged leaves to facilitate harvesting the smaller regrowth of new leaves.

Mizuna looks ragged through winter but if it survives there will be new, delicate leaves in March and early April, before the arrival of some tasty flowering shoots.

Mustard

Varieties: Mustards offer a most interesting range of leaves, with strong flavours and beautiful appearance. *Red Frills* and *Green Frills* (also called *Ruby Streaks* and *Golden Streaks*) are the mildest and most attractive mustards for salad, with lots of tender feathers on each leaf. *Green in the Snow* is hardiest for midwinter, when its extremely pungent leaves are smaller. I particularly like the *Frills* varieties for milder flavour and good looks. *Red Giant* is better for large, stir-fry leaves.

Sow: July to September

Space: As for mizuna

Harvest: August onwards. *Red Frills* turns crimson in cooler weather.

Harvest by regular removal of larger stems. Cutting *Frills* varieties is possible but shortens the harvest period. *Green in the Snow* lives longest, while *Red Frills* is usually first to flower. Many mustards can be kept producing over long periods by careful picking of larger leaves, and I do this all through winter in the polytunnel so as to keep the same plants healthy and productive from November until late April.

Mustards in December: for salads (left), and white mustard for green manure (right), which also has edible tips!

Mustard *Red Lace*. Fennel (foreground) has tasty leaves too.

Pak choi

Varieties: *Tai Sai* for long leaves, *Green Revolution* and *Joi Choi F1* for short, fat ones, *Red Lady F1* for purple ones
Sow: Late July to August
Space: 25x25cm (10x10") for larger leaves, 25x5cm for smaller leaves (10x2")
Harvest: August to early October
Pak choi starts promisingly, producing attractive leaves with thick white stems – and then is suddenly full of slug holes, or being eaten by caterpillars and flea beetles. I find it as difficult as Chinese cabbage but sow it more often because leaves are ready about four weeks after sowing in August, and young ones are delicious in salads.

There is a range of colours, shapes and leaf thickness, according to the variety grown. They resist frost but are not usually winter-hardy outside, so are best grown in a greenhouse or polytunnel through the winter, as long as you are in control of slugs. *Joi Choi* is my favourite, while *Tai Sai* is easier to pick with its longer, thinner leaves. All varieties can also be cut.

Tatsoi

Varieties: *Rozetta F1* and *Yukina Savoy* for large leaves and long stems
Sow: August
Space: As for mizuna
Harvest: September to October
Similar to its rhyming relative pak choi but usually smaller-leaved and more

Pak choi *Joi Choi F1* for stir-fry leaves, has been picked once.

compact, with less stem. Shorter-stemmed varieties have lovely glossy leaves but are more difficult to pick; cutting is more realistic for them. Frost-hardiness is good and some reasonable leaves can be had in March and April, particularly if some shelter is given.

Rockets

There are many variations on the main two types: larger-leaved salad rocket and thin-leaved wild rocket. They both grow in a similar way to oriental brassica leaves, but wild rocket is perennial.
Sow: Late July to mid-September
Space: 20x5cm (8x2") sown in rows, or 20x20cm (8x8") for multi-sown clumps
Harvest: August onwards

Salad rocket and wild rocket

Salad rocket offers higher yields and milder flavours than wild rocket, with a range of varietal choice. My best results are from standard salad rocket offered by Bingenheim Saatgut (see Resources). The leaves of wild rocket are thinner, darker and more serrated, and its flowers are yellow rather than white.

Harvest by cutting or by picking larger leaves. I prefer to pick salad rocket, and cut wild rocket. Flowering stems appear in early autumn from summer sowings; keep removing them to encourage more leaves. In spring, salad rocket flowers persistently and leaf production diminishes to small amounts by early May, whereas wild rocket comes into its own, giving excellent harvests from

167

April to July. I pull it out in July, before the flowers set seed as it can become a weed. Best harvests of wild rocket are from new sowings in August.

Here is another variation - Wasabi rocket, which is not true Wasabi, but is a cheap and quick way to have some of that Wasabi-like, horseradish flavour in leaves that look like normal rocket, just a little smaller and pale.

Other brassicas

Kale

Although there are many kinds of kale, only a few grow tender leaves to enjoy in salad, unless they are eaten as baby plants (see Chapter 4, pages 38-49). Kale's winter hardiness and profusion of tender flowering shoots in spring are valuable assets.

Varieties: *Red Russian* leaves are tender and tasty in salads. They are a pretty mauve colour with serrated margins. Small leaves of *Nero di Toscana* (Black Cabbage or *Cavolo Nero*) have rich flavour and colour. Small leaves of perennial kale such as Daubenton are tasty in salad.

Pigeons may mean you need a net or mesh cover. Another pest is gall midges, which eat out the growing points in early summer. However, plants recover by making new growing points, whose small leaves are good for salads.

Option 1: Spacing/growing for large plants
Sow: Late June to mid-July
Space: 40x40cm (16x16")
Harvest: October to May

If your plants make it to autumn in good shape, you can enjoy some of the lower leaves, cooked if they are large, while leaving all the small ones to fuel future growth. Medium-sized leaves can be chopped and eaten raw in winter. Then as winter draws to a close, new shoots with plenty of small leaves appear at different points on the stem, and by April these will be making flower buds. All of this new growth is delicious raw. Finally, by May the new stems become thinner and tougher.

Option 2: Spacing/growing for baby plants
Sow: Mid-July to early August more thickly
Space: 25x5cm (10x2") or 20x20cm (8x8") for multi-sown modules, for harvests from mid-August
Harvest: August to May

Small leaves can be picked off from mid- to late August and regularly thereafter. Plants will be small going into winter but no less hardy for that and should provide more small leaves in late winter and until early May.

One bad pest in spring can be grey aphids, which suck sap out of new leaves until they shrivel. This happens particularly after mild winters, just when plants look in good shape. Washing with soapy water or just water is the best answer.

Cabbages

Most leaves of European cabbages are a little tough and waxy for use in salads, but see Chapter 4, pages 38-49 for ideas on growing them as micro leaves.

Kohlrabi

Sow: July-August
Space: 20x5cm (8x2") sown in rows or 20x20cm (8x8") for multi-sown clumps
Harvest: August to November
Some kohlrabis have been bred for fast-growing, tender leaves of green or purple hue. Their leaves resist flea beetle a little, and the purple-leaved variety is worth a try for its waxy, almost translucent hues of purple and pink.

Rape

Sow: August to mid-September
Space: As for kohlrabi or closer, 15x2cm (6x1") for baby leaves
Harvest: September to May
Rape is fast-growing, and like cabbage, its salad leaves want eating small. It is especially suitable for growing as micro or baby leaves (see Chapter 4), or for sowing more thickly to cut baby leaves when young.

Texel greens

Sow: July to September
Space: As for kohlrabi or wider, 30x30cm (12x12") for large plants
Harvest: August onwards
A farmer once expressed amazement that I was growing Texel greens to eat, since he thought it was only good for pheasants, and it is certainly not well-known as a salad ingredient. Yet its leaves are tender, mild, fast-growing, and frost-hardy. When given more room the plants grow 60cm (2') high or more, with large leaves that are tasty as cooked greens.

Turnips for leaves

Varieties: *Rapa Senza Testa* for abundant leaf shoots
Sow: March to April or August to mid-September
Space: As for rape
Harvest: From three to four weeks after sowing
Young turnip leaves are pale green, hairy and tender, with a pleasant mild flavour. Closely spaced plants can be cut over two or three times and picking the odd leaf off turnips grown for roots does not discourage their growth. Also there are turnip varieties that have been bred for more leaves and less root, such as *Rapa Senza Testa,* and if allowed to grow large they are good as cooked greens.

CHAPTER FOURTEEN

SPINACH, CHARD AND BEET

MANY COLOURS, STRONG FLAVOURS

Brief summary

* Leaves of strong flavour, best picked small.

* Sow spinach from February indoors and March outdoors, until August, best to avoid sowing in May and June.

* Indoor sowings in modules are less at risk from slugs and woodlice.

* Sow red, yellow, pink and/or white chard and beet in April, then one more sowing in June should ensure leaves until mid-autumn.

* Spinach produces its tastiest leaves in the spring but is always at risk from slugs.

* Chard is less delicate but still of interest to slugs.

* Harvest larger leaves by hand or all leaves by knife.

* Removal of flowering stems will prolong the useful life of plants.

* Spinach sown in summer can survive winter to give a new crop of delicious leaves in spring. Chard is also reasonably winter-hardy.

A month after interplanting spinach, herbs, endive and brassicas between lettuce – see page 175.

Spinach, chard and beetroot all belong to the same sub-family of Chenopodiaceae. They are descendants of wild sea beets which have been bred in different directions, chard for its colourful and fleshy stalks, beet for its roots, and spinach for its more tender leaves. In the Middle East, spinach is called 'Prince of Vegetables' for its rich flavour and delicate texture.

It has become common in Britain to eat these leaves in salads, when they are small enough to retain a mild flavour without the acidity and rather aggressive tastes found in larger leaves when raw. Chard and beets are best used for the pretty colours of their stems and veins, which alter in each season. The leaves are paler in summer, then turn darker in winter.

I find that small chard and beet leaves rarely excite the palate, but spinach definitely can. Its flavour varies through the year, according to both season and weather, reaching a zenith of rich sweetness in the spring, when it is most in season. Freshly gathered small leaves from young plants also possess a lovely succulence.

NORMAL PATTERN OF GROWTH

Spinach

Temperatures of -8 to 10°C (down to 14°F) do not trouble spinach; it's hardier than those soft leaves suggest. Such resistance to cold, allied to spring flowering, means that seed is best to germinate in late summer and grow into plants large enough to survive the winter; it then grows again in spring and makes plenty of seed by early summer. Seeding also happens in the same year and much more quickly from spring sowing. Regular picking of spring leaves can slow this process, but August sowing is best for enjoying long periods of harvest.

Chard

This follows a similar pattern to spinach, except it flowers a little earlier, so a sowing in late spring can give leaves all summer and autumn. Green chard or leaf beet (cooking spinach) can also be grown for baby leaves. Summer sowings that survive the winter will flower by the following spring.

Beetroot

Beetroot grown for leaves and regularly picked will eventually make a small root that is edible, but tougher and less sweet than ordinary beetroots. As with chard, these roots flower after winter if frosts have not been severe enough to kill them.

SOWING

The two seasons of salad spinach – spring (from April to early June) and autumn (September to November) – are covered by two or three sowings a month before in each case: February/March and early August. Chard requires only two sowings in April and July, and beet only needs one sowing in April for continuous leaves.

When sowing direct, aim for about a

Salads of spinach and kale (front), sorrel and chard (under fleece), mustards and rocket (back).

seed every centimetre (two or three per inch) in rows 20-25cm (8-10") apart. Seeds are of a fair size and easy to handle. For module-sowing, three seeds per cell gives a clump of medium-sized leaves; plant at 15-20cm (6-8").

The earliest harvests from March onwards come from sowings made in late summer, between mid-July and mid-August; these give autumn leaves too. It is also possible to make early sowings of spinach in February in a greenhouse with gentle heat, then plant under fleece in late March or early April. Chard is better sown later, from mid-April and in May, to reduce the risk of flowering. They are then cropping in June and July, just when spinach prefers to make a flowering stem.

GROWING

If seed comes up more thickly than suggested above, it pays to thin them out so that you have fewer, stronger plants rather than many spindly ones.

Water in dry spells, especially spinach, whose tendency to run to seed in late spring and summer can be delayed for a while by keeping its roots moist.

CONTAINER GROWING

Spinach for small salad leaves grows well in containers and can still grow into large leaves. In early spring, for example, you can pick off its baby leaves for a month or so, when most appreciated, and then allow it to grow rapidly in May warmth – with plenty of watering – for a final crop of leaves to cook (see recipe in Chapter 10, page 109). Chard is equally versatile and all the beets do well in containers.

PESTS

Slugs like these leaves and require your normal methods of control.

Sparrows like red beet leaves and chard, and make many small holes: cover with netting if this happens. Bird damage shows as several jagged holes rather than slugs' more random and larger ones. Spinach seedlings are a favourite meal of woodlice, common in many gardens and often colonizing new beds and pots after a few months. Woodlice nibble the edges of leaves on the ground, and more annoyingly the baby leaves of spinach, after which those leaves grow ragged. It helps to sow spinach in non-woody compost and to maintain the propagating area free of rotting wood. This helps control slug numbers too (also see box, right).

HARVESTING LEAVES

Young leaves hold all the aces – tender, tasty, pretty – so it is worth picking regularly. A knife can be used to cut across the tops of plants, but always taking care to cut above the smallest visible leaf. The next cut will be ready later than if leaves had been picked off. Small spinach leaves are better picked than cut because of their more prostrate habit, with leaves growing horizontally outwards, so that by the time you might have gathered them up to cut their stems, they can have been carefully

A BETTER MOOD IN THE GARDEN

As well as harvesting all good leaves, it is worth removing any yellowing or eaten ones to decrease food and hiding areas for slugs. The appearance of the plant is also improved and this is psychologically important, helping to keep you enthusiastic and happy with your garden.

picked. When picking, it helps to have a good thumbnail for pinching the stalk, to avoid root disturbance.

As flowering stems appear, keep pinching or cutting them to promote more leaf growth. With chard and beet, the harvest can be prolonged over two extra months or more, but spinach leaves become smaller and more bitter soon after a flowering tendency begins, especially from May to early July, when they quickly go out of season. Sometime in late autumn, new growth will almost cease and although plants continue to grow slowly in any mild winter weather, there is only a small amount of harvestable leaves until the arrival of some early spring warmth.

VARIETIES

The following varieties have given me good results. There are many others worth trying and new ones come along all the time.

Charles planting spinach after clearing wild rocket, late August.

Interplanting spinach between lettuce, late August.

August plants of spinach, ready 16 days from sowing: *Palco F1* (left), *Medania* (right).

Spinach *Fiorano F1*
Extremely fast to produce mid-green and round leaves, rising to flower quite quickly as well, so best suited to little and frequent sowings for two or three quick cuts of baby leaves. *Fiorana* may also survive the winter from sowing in early August.

Spinach *Medania*
One of the hardiest varieties for over-wintering, and open-pollinated so you can save seeds, unlike the *F1* varieties. The dark, thick leaves are of excellent flavour raw, even when large and especially after cold weather, when they become impressively sweet. Sow late July to mid-August, and again late winter.

Spinach *Red Kitten F1*
This variety is tricky to grow because it seeds readily from early sowings; it is best to wait until early August before sowing. However, the wait is worth-while as its red-stemmed, pointed leaves are attractive and of good flavour.

Spinach *Palco F1*
An excellent variety for early leaves that are round and quite thick, light green in colour and of fair flavour. Often available as organic seed.

Spinach *Yukon F1*
Fast-growing and with more pointed, dark green leaves that can also be left to grow really large for cooking. An upright habit of growth makes picking easier.

Medania spinach at the new year – it's very hardy.

A fleece cover helped *Boltardy* beetroot to grow in a cold April. It was sown late February in modules.

Tree spinach

An unusual variant, growing 60-90cm (24-36") high on a slightly woody stem, with many new shoots of glowing magenta leaves at their centre; leaves are more purple on their undersides. If sown in early spring, the plants become truly tree like, up to 2m (6') high with an abundance of leaves and shoots. Shoots are best for salad and leave pink dust on your fingers after picking. Large leaves are tougher and best cooked, until late summer when flowering stems replace new leaves. It is best to remove plants at this stage, before they drop seeds everywhere – tree spinach is related to fat hen (*Chenopodium album*), which produces an abundance of seed.

Chard *Bright Yellow*

Yellow chard grows a little more quickly than ruby chard and has pretty, luminous stems that add zestful colour to a bowl of mixed leaves.

Chard *Bright Lights*

Usually sold as *Rainbow,* this is a mixture of different coloured chards from red to orange to pink to yellow to white, often with more of the pale colours, which tend to grow more vigorously than highly coloured leaves. So if you want richly coloured chards, it is better to buy varieties of named colour such as *Ruby. Bright Lights* has stronger colours and is an excellent choice for random plants of different sizes, some to cook and some to eat raw.

Chard *Ruby, Vulcan*

These red-stemmed chards are a selection of bold colour and look as attractive in the garden as on the plate.

Beet *Bull's Blood*

This variety has lovely dark stems and

Spring plantings of coriander, spring onions and beetroot for leaves.

even its leaves are more ruby than green, especially in cooler weather. Sow in April and pick leaves until October or later, watching the baby beetroot grow as well! When leaves are regularly picked, the beetroot are less sweet to eat, but they are tasty roots when leaves are not picked.

Beet *Red Titan F1*

Another beet with strikingly dark crimson stems and thinner leaves than chards, but this variety does have some green leaf between its red veins and a good flavour.

Leaf beet *Erbette*

Leaf beet has thinner stems than chard, of a pale green colour. *Erbette* has a better flavour for eating raw than most leaf beets and it survives winter a little better than most chards, with reasonable regrowth of pale green, quite fleshy leaves in early spring.

CHAPTER FIFTEEN

EXOTIC TASTES AND COLOURS

SMALL AMOUNTS OF LARGE FLAVOURS

Brief summary

* Baby plants and shoots of many vegetables have appealing flavour, but avoid the poisonous solanums (nightshades) – potato, tomato, aubergine and pepper.

* Pea shoots are always popular: sow closer than usual and keep pinching out all growing points.

* Broad bean plants can be treated like peas; their shoots have a stronger, less sweet flavour.

* Other possibilities are young carrot tops, fennel leaves, celeriac, broccoli and asparagus.

* Summer purslane is in its own idiosyncratic category of succulent, lemony, drought-resistant leaves.

* For striking colours, try small leaves of amaranth, orache, red perilla and others from previous chapters, such as red beet, lettuce and basil. See Chapter 4, pages 47-9 for more ideas on growing baby vegetable leaves in small spaces.

Gladioli, amaranth now seeding and lettuce behind.

You can grow exciting tastes and colours from plants that are not difficult to grow. The yields of leaves and shoots may be small, but the flavours and colours are so vivid that only a small quantity is needed to give great character to salad dishes.

NORMAL PATTERN OF GROWTH

A wide range of plant types are covered here, so few generalizations can be made. Peas, beans, orache and tree spinach will set seed by the end of summer, while many of the other vegetables will grow quite large if allowed to, with leaves that become too tough for salad. Regular harvesting at the right moment is important.

SOWING

Most of these plants should be sown between March and July, and have special seasons when they grow best – check dates for each one. Two sowings, early and late, will give a longer period of harvest.

HARVESTING

The quantities from these plants are mostly small and regular, usually after a slow start in spring. When you pinch off the tip from a small pea plant it looks pretty terminal, and for a while nothing more grows. Yet the stem elongates and new shoots appear; harvest these after 10 days and there will be even more on several new stems, for many more weeks.

Autumn: *Red Lace* mustard is flowering before other salads. The flowers and stem tops are edible.

Charles removing seeding orache to sow winter mustard in September.

Since most leaves for colour are of average flavour, sometimes strong and bitter when large, they are best picked small. This encourages growth of more small leaves, and flowering is delayed over a long period.

CONTAINER GROWING

All plants in this chapter work in containers, and the coloured ones such as amaranth and orache look really attractive as well. Peas and beans require larger pots or tubs, because they can grow big and bushy after three months or more. Module-sowing works well for planting into containers; if sowing direct you will need to modify the spacings since rows are not appropriate. Closer spacings work well in pots filled with good compost: for example the fennel spacing of 15x5cm, can become one seed every 5cm (2") in all directions.

VEGETABLES FOR SHOOTS AND TIPS

This section is for regular pickings of shoots and tips. See also Chapter 4, pages 47-9 for sowing many of the same vegetables more thickly in shallow trays, for quick harvests of tiny leaves.

Asparagus

Not many people eat raw asparagus but I often snack on a spear or two when picking, and love the snappy tastes and texture. Chop two or three spears into

Pea shoots (front) and the beauty of Homeacres garden in June.

small pieces to add crunch and flavour to many salads in spring and early summer.

Broad beans

As with peas, the growing tip of each plant is the initial harvest, after which the growth of new shoots is less prodigious. The flavour is less appealing than peas, nicely 'beany' but also earthy and strong. Flower buds sometimes come with the harvested tips and these are excellent to eat, offering a more delicate taste of broad bean. Or harvest flowers from close-sown beans.

Sowing, growing

For salad harvests, space seeds at 15x5cm (6x2"). Sow in November and again in February to May.

Harvesting

The growing point can be pinched out when plants are about 45cm (18") high. For harvests of pods, wait until May or June, depending on when you sowed, for plants to become covered in flowers and some baby pods at the bottom, then pinch out their growing points. New stems will often appear from the same roots and their growing tips can again be pinched out.

As well as giving you a tasty harvest, removing the top cluster of small leaves and flowers has two extra benefits: it encourages faster development of broad beans and makes it harder for black aphids to establish themselves, as they like to arrive and develop in the tight cluster of baby leaves if you have not harvested them for salad! The bean tops, lightly steamed, also make a tasty green vegetable.

Once pods are growing, plants put all their energy in that direction and new shoots become hard to find.

Bulb fennel

The extremities of the feathery, fern-like leaves of bulb fennel are tender in salad and if you enjoy minty, aniseed flavours you will appreciate them. Bulb fennel is an umbellifer, like carrot, and its edible roots carry a noticeable taste of carrot. It is good value because all of the plant can be eaten, although the roots are fibrous, and fiddly to prepare.

Sowing

From May to August, direct in the soil at 15x5cm (6x2") or at four seeds per module, which are later planted at 12x12cm (5x5").

Growing and harvesting

Fennel is small and spindly at first; wait until plants are about 15cm (6") high before pinching out the growing point of a leaf or two and some feathery leaf edges. Keep picking for many weeks and then small bulbs will form and are good to eat before flowering stems develop, when plants should be pulled up.

Sowings in July and August are unlikely to flower and best left to bulb up, without picking any leaves until the final harvest in October or November. At this point the leaf tips are especially welcome, when harvests of salad leaves are generally smaller.

Carrot

Carrot seedlings no more than 7-10cm (3-4") high, have a sweet flavour and are tender as well. Larger carrot tops have little hairs, making their outer surface rougher, and fibres to stiffen their stalks. To eat larger carrot leaves, either sow a hairless variety that has been bred for use as salad leaves and possesses a fine carrot flavour, if you can find some seed, or chop carrot leaves as fine as possible.

Sowing

From March to August, direct at 15x3cm (6x1"), or four to six seeds per module to plant at 8x8cm (3x3").

Growing and harvesting

Early growth is slow but once plants are about 10cm (4") high, a few sprigs of leaves can be pinched off at intervals for a month or two. Roots will be small and barely edible when leaves are regularly trimmed back, also because of close spacings.

Celeriac and celery

The young leaves and leaf tips of these vegetables have powerful, bitter tastes that combine parsley and celery (see also parcel, page 202). I do not recommend growing celery and celeriac espe-

Multi-sown clumps of peas at 22cm (9") spacing make a forest of pea shoots after four harvests.

cially for their leaves, but if they are in the garden anyway, a few leaf tips can be pinched as they grow.

Peas

Almost any variety of pea can be used, but tall varieties have more vigour and their longer shoots are easier to pick. I grow *Alderman* and *Tall Sugar*, and always allow a few to mature in order to save their seeds. Not all pea seed that you buy is as fresh as it might be, resulting in poor germination, so I do recommend keeping your own, if you have room in the garden, to allow a few pea pods to dry on the vine.

Sowing

From February to April is the best time for sowing, and you have until July to sow more, although late sowings grow less vigorously and healthily. A well-tended and regularly picked March sowing can last through the main season of pea shoots, which is May and June; while a sowing in May will give less shoots for half the number of weeks, because the plants want to flower in summer. Another issue in summer is that leaf mildew can become prevalent after mid-July, especially in dry weather, so you need to water more in dry summers. Pea plants like damp conditions.

There are many ways of sowing pea seeds:

* Directly into soil from mid-March until early May: Either dib holes 2-3cm (1") deep and 15-20cm (6-8") apart, dropping three or four seeds in each, or draw out drills 25cm (10") apart and drop in about 25 seeds per metre (i.e. 1½" apart).
* Indoors from mid-February to April: Sow three or four seeds per module, for planting out after about three weeks, when seedlings are 5cm (2") high, using the same spacing as above.
* In a plastic gutter of compost: Sow peas every 2cm (1"), grow them under cover, then slide them into a shallow trough in the soil when of similar size to module-grown peas; the gutter must be smooth and shiny.
* In containers: One or two seeds at an equidistant spacing of 5-10cm (2-4"), for harvests after a month for three to five weeks, depending on variety and picking method.

Sowing indoors can help in safeguarding seed from hungry birds and mice. However, even in the greenhouse you may need a mousetrap primed all spring, because one rodent can eat a lot of potential harvests in a night.

Growing

If your garden or outdoor space is bothered by birds (such as pigeons and rooks) interested in eating or just pulling out young pea plants, cover plants with fleece or mesh for about a month, by which time the birds should be finding enough to eat elsewhere. Fleece also helps them to grow in cool spring weather: I lay it directly on plants and they push it up for the first four weeks after transplanting.

Harvesting

When plants are 20-30cm (8-12") high, pinch or cut off their top 5-7cm (2-3") and enjoy the early flavour of pea, with all its promise of summer to come. You may then have to wait another fortnight or more before the next shoots are ready, and thereafter keep picking them at the length you most enjoy. Baby shoots are the most tender; longer shoots give more to eat and even their tendrils are edible, but a little tougher.

Eventually shoots will develop flowers of a lovely pea flavour, so you have many choices for different salads. If you are growing peas for pods, they often carry a surplus of flowers and the pea harvest will not be diminished by picking a few of these to eat. You could also pick their main, and then perhaps secondary, shoots once fully grown.

Conversely, peas grown for salad often manage to set a few pods on shoots which were missed, so a small harvest of peas can be enjoyed in summer as the production of new shoots slows down. New stems become thinner, spindly and rather tough after about two months of picking from the same plant. So pull them up for the compost heap and then, after removing your plants, there is still half the season left to grow another fine salad crop.

For more on growing peas and pea shoots, see the video on my website www.charlesdowding.co.uk.

Turnip leaves are tasty too.

Salsola (also called Salsola soda, Okahijiki, land seaweed or Saltwort)

A succulent plant of unusual salty flavour and crunchy texture. For eating in salad, shoots must be young and tender. They can also be lightly steamed or stir-fried, offering a mild flavour and unusual spikiness.

Sowing

Sow from May to July, allowing about 15cm (6") between plants.

Harvesting

After six to eight weeks you can pinch off shoots about 2-3cm (1") long. If plants are kept well watered, they will then keep producing more tender shoots for up to two months. Eventually the stems become tougher as flowering commences.

Summer purslane

This plant requires heat, sun and dry air, rather like basil. Therefore moist, oceanic summers, with the constant humidity and regular rainfall that is ideal for, say, lettuce, have a bad effect on summer purslane, turning its round, succulent leaves to a paler-than-usual colour with browning at the edges. However, a superb, lemony flavour and crisp succulence of the leaves make it worth a try every year.

Sowing

Draw shallow drills for the tiny seeds and be wary of dropping too many in. Rows about 20-25cm (8-10") apart will allow for plants to grow and keep growing.

Golden purslane is best sown from mid-June to late July and crops for less time than green purslane.

Green purslane can be sown between early June and early August, growing larger and cropping for longer than golden purslane. Three sowings in early June, July and August should give leaves for most of a hot summer.

Harvesting

When plants are about 10cm (4") high, the first shoots can be gathered, pinching all tender stems around the plants' edges. Shoots are normally about 3cm (1") long with about eight or ten leaves and a tender stem.

Then keep picking any new stems every few days – there will be noticeably more in hot weather. Watch out for seed pods that appear almost invisibly, hidden under some topmost leaves; they are the same colour as the leaves but with a bitter flavour.

Golden purslane may crop for only three weeks before making bitter seed pods but individual leaves can still be picked for a while after that.

Green purslane produces tender new shoots for up to six weeks, depending on conditions, and is higher yielding than golden purslane. Their flavours are similar.

Turnip

In Britain this was probably the best-known brassica for leaf harvests, before the arrival of so many interesting plants from the Orient. Small leaves are best, before they grow hairy and fibrous.

Sowing

Sow direct or in modules, four to six seeds per module for planting as a clump, from March to mid-April and again in August to mid-September, using the same spacings as for carrots. Cover spring sowings and plantings with fleece, to speed growth and reduce damage from flea beetles.

Growing and harvesting

Growth is rapid and leaves can be picked or cut off once the first true leaves are formed; a month after sowing in spring and less than three weeks after sowing in late summer. Continued cutting of leaves slows root growth, but if plants are thinned to about 10cm (4") apart after two or three leaf harvests, some small turnips can develop.

Spring harvests finish by the end of May, as flowering time approaches. That makes leaves tough and with holes too, from flea beetle.

September: (from front) French marigold, chicory and chard under mesh to protect from sparrows. Bulb fennel and mustards are in the bed on the right.

MICRO SOWINGS OF OTHER VEGETABLES

Many small vegetable plants can be eaten whole, for the flavours in both their baby leaves and tender, juicy stems. Cabbages, broccoli, parsnips, onions, leeks and others lend themselves to sowing in seed trays, window-boxes or whatever you can lay your hands on – see Chapter 4, pages 47-9 for more details.

PAINTING WITH LEAVES

Some plants have such a depth of pigment that their appearance among other vegetables can bring a fine touch of fiery exuberance and exoticism. I love to grow them as much for their exciting looks outside as for the colour lift they bring to bowls of salad leaves.

Amaranth (also called Chinese spinach or Bayam Callaloo)

The many names of amaranth reflect its common uses across non-English speaking cultures.

Sowing

Amaranth likes warmth so wait until mid-May or June to sow, at similar spacings to bulb fennel on page 185. One sowing may do for the summer, or perhaps sow again in mid-July. If it is hot, there are larger leaves and a more rapid tendency to flower and seed.

Growing and harvesting

Be prepared for quite slow growth in a cool summer, which at least helps to keep the leaves small. Larger leaves are more leathery, less appropriate for salad and with an unexciting, flat flavour. So keep picking the small leaves of striking colour – the variety *Garnet Red* has a gorgeous ruby tone to the underside of its leaves. Seeds produced at summer's end can be knocked out and kept for sowing, and are nutritious to eat – if a lot of work to prepare on a small scale.

Orache (also called Atriplex or Mountain spinach)

There are many names for this plant which is also known as 'red fat hen', an informative name, revealing its similarity to the well-known weed. Indeed if left to seed it will reappear for years to come. Another relative is tree spinach (page 178); both are for colour more than flavour.

Sowing

Sow from March to June, using the same spacings as for bulb fennel on page 185. Sowings in early spring crop for longest, and at a more useful time of year.

Growing and harvesting

Leaves have a striking colour right from the beginning, and a few small leaves may be gathered when plants are only 7-10cm (3-4") high. Harvests increase steadily, and any flowering shoots can also be eaten when young. Then after a couple of months or so, the tiny flowers and seeds become more numerous than new leaves, best to remove plants at this stage. Perhaps allow one to grow for seed, which takes another month, and it may grow as high as 1m (4').

Red basil

For details on growing this see the next chapter, pages 195-8. I mention it here because the deep hue and density of its leaves stands out beautifully in a mix of salad leaves. Colour is the sole reason for growing it, because the flavour is ordinary and can even be bitter.

Red perilla

The dark red, crinkled leaves of this Japanese herb have both looks and flavour, but the latter is strong and spicy – not to everybody's taste in salads.

Sowing

Sow in May or June as it grows better in heat.

Harvesting

Keep picking small leaves from about a month of sowing and see how you like it!

CHAPTER SIXTEEN

HERBS AND FLOWERS

MORE EXCITING FLAVOURS AND COLOURS

Brief summary

* Herbs are not difficult to grow, and enrich salads with deep reservoirs of flavour and nutrition, beautiful textures and some vivid colours.

* Parsley is almost a year-round herb, but other annual herbs have seasons, so check for their best sowing times.

* By careful picking you can prolong the useful life of many herbs and keep them producing tender leaves.

Herbs such as chervil and flat leaved parsley are so much more than a garnish: full of flavour, and rich in vitamin C too. There are many herbal possibilities for adding to salads, as well as other dishes. A garden or patio with one plant each of parsley, basil, sorrel, coriander and chervil – but in different seasons (see below, pages 195-207) – gives you small and frequent harvests of rich flavour over weeks and months.

Flowers are another source of intriguing variety and colour, and not only the obvious ones like nasturtium and marigold. Some herb flowers have a wonderful flavour – garlic chives and coriander, for instance – as do baby ornamental flowers such as heartsease, and large ones like sunflowers.

Basil Lime (below) and *Sweet Genovese* (above), after picking 2kg (4lb 6oz) of shoots.

Scabious, nasturtium and marigolds with kale in autumn.

HERBS

Normal pattern of growth

The herbs covered here range from tender annuals (basil), which flower and die by the season's end, through biennials (parsley), which flower in their second year, to hardy perennials (chives), which grow from the same roots year after year. The flowers here (see pages 205-7) are mostly annuals that set flowers over a reasonably long period, before and sometimes at the same time as setting seed, so they grow again the following year from their own seeds.

Sowing

Both modules and small pots of 5cm (2") diameter work well for sowing clumps of herb and flower seeds. Set these clumps of seedlings into larger pots, beds or borders when their first true leaves are well established. Different herbs are ready to plant at different stages – check the descriptions below.

Spacing

Similar spacings work for many herbs; around 25x10cm (10x4") for direct sowing in rows or 20x20cm (8x8") when planting modules. Multi-sown, module-raised herbs can be grown as clumps for harvests of small leaves, or thinned to individual plants at the same spacings for harvests of larger leaves.

Basil (tender annual)

All basils are tender annuals, killed by even a slight frost. To grow good basil, remember two simple things: it needs warmth and dislikes too much moisture on its leaves. Imagine it growing on an Italian hillside in full sun and with occasional summer storms, and aim for a habitat like that in your garden!

In a cloudy summer, basil struggles and requires protection from regular cold rain: outdoor growing is difficult in an oceanic climate, and succeeds only in hot summers. Otherwise, grow basil in a greenhouse, polytunnel, conservatory or even on the window sill.

Basil comes in many delicious and pretty varieties, which offer a spectrum of rich flavours and leaf types.

Container growing

All plants covered here grow well in containers and can make you a nearly instant herb garden wherever is most convenient. If they grow more leaves than you require, it is better to keep plants on the small side by picking off and composting larger leaves. This keeps plants tidy, reduces slug numbers, means less watering and draws less nutrients out of the compost. Slugs can be an issue with tender basil, so avoid planting it outside before about mid-June.

Basil *Sweet Genovese*, harvested twice.

Sowing

Outdoor sowing is for warm weather only – say, from early summer – and means a long wait for harvests. Basil can be sown under cover any time in spring, from early April (with warmth) to early June. Sow in a seed tray to prick out after two weeks, or two or five seeds per module.

Basil seedlings often damp off in soggy compost, so a heated propagator is an especially good way to get it going. Add 50 per cent vermiculite/perlite to the compost, to improve drainage and have more air around the roots. Water sparingly, often every two to three days, as the tiny seedlings grow slowly unless it is sunny. In cloudy weather, their roots are happier in partially dry compost.

Growing

When seed tray seedlings have two to four leaves, prick them into modules or very small pots. Basil can be grown either as individual plants or as clumps of three or four together. Handle seedlings gently by the leaves only, so as not to squash their fragile stems.

Around a month or more after sowing, when your plants are 5-7cm (2-3") high, pop them into a slightly larger pot for another two or three weeks, at the end of which time they can be set in their final summer location.

In the ground, set plants (single or multi-sown) at 22cm (9"), which allows space for new growth and harvests all summer.

Likewise, one or more plants in a 25-30cm (10-12") pot can grow to a good size, indoors or in a sunny place outside, and may be sufficient for most households. Since you need only a few plants, it may be viable to buy them, except that nurseries may not offer the varieties you want.

Harvesting

By the start of summer, you should be able to gather a shoot or two, and then more each week as your plants become established. The best time to harvest new shoots, by pinching or cutting, is before any flowering when, in place of new baby leaves, you see a stem and tiny flower buds.

After each harvest, new shoots with growing leaves appear just below the points of removal, then after a while they also tend to flower and should be picked in the same way. Soon you have a small bush covered in new growth.

Each variety has different patterns of growth and best results come from harvesting when most new leaves and shoots are happening. Sometimes it is easier to use a knife, for example with the small shoots of *Greek* basil, which can be treated as though they are the extremities of a mini-hedge and trimmed accordingly, cutting about 1cm (half an inch) of new growth each fortnight or three weeks.

Through September there will be a gradual loss of leaf quality and occasional mouldy leaves and stems: best to pick these off to compost. Keeping plants clean helps prolong their productive life into October, until it turns too dark and cool for healthy new leaves to develop.

Charles planting dill and coriander in early spring.

Problems

Raising plants is a challenge: don't sow too early and don't overwater. Most difficulties in growing are cause by cool, damp weather, which results in browning of the leaves, pale weak stems and a susceptibility to attack by slugs. Growing plants in good light and warmth, in fertile free-draining soil or compost gives plentiful harvests of healthy leaves. In hot weather, you can give plenty pos water because plants are growing so fast. Then by early autumn, conditions change so leaves and stems go more mouldy with every week. Best to replant with a winter herb such as chervil.

Varieties

I recommend trying some of each, perhaps over a couple of years, for a taste of the exciting range of flavours and growth habits on offer.

Cinnamon

Grows up to 50cm high, with good-sized leaves of spicy flavour. Plants readily make stems of dark red flowers, which need pinching out often to ensure new leaf production.

Genovese or Sweet

The most productive and easy-to-grow variety, best for making pesto too. Large numbers of rounded, glossy leaves grow to a fair size in warm conditions. Plants grow large and tall, with less tendency to flower than many other varieties.

Broad-leaved sorrel and parsley overwintered outside, then covered with a fleece in mid-February.

Greek

A mound-like plant with masses of tiny light green leaves, which you can shave off in clumps with a knife or scissors. It makes a pretty pot plant and grows large if there is plenty of sun and warmth, and there is less tendency to flower than most other basils.

Lemon

The leaves live up to their name flavor-wise, being intense and citrus-like. Their texture is soft and tender and a few of these can liven up many salads or dishes of cooked food. A notable tendency to flower means that it must be regularly picked.

Lettuce leaf

Lettuce leaf is one of the largest-leaved varieties but is quick to flower and its leaves are prone to fungal infections. Best in drier climates.

Lime

The leaves of *lime* basil are smaller, firmer, glossier and more numerous than lemon basil, with an even more pronounced citric aroma and tangy flavour. When frequently picked, it can grow into a dense bush of 35cm (14") or more.

Red

This pretty variety boasts extremely dark ruby-coloured leaves, grows more slowly than most green basils, and has rather less flavour, with a touch of bitterness.

Sweet Thai

Sweet Thai is a spicy variety, with hints of aniseed and cloves, and it shows a willingness to break out in colourful mauve flowers. Worth growing under cover rather than outside.

Chervil (hardy annual/ biennial)

Chervil is almost exactly the opposite of basil in terms of its climatic and seasonal requirements, because it thrives on dampness. As a winter herb it offers so much: steady growth in low light levels, frost resistance and a flavour of mild aniseed. When I give taste samples to people, they are always impressed.

Sowing

To have maximum leaves for least effort, I recommend sowing in late summer, mainly August. Slow growth at first makes module-sowing worthwhile: three or four seeds per module to grow together in a clump. Or sow in a seed tray to prick out after two weeks, one per module, which makes picking easier if you want individual stems.

Sowing in spring gives small harvests before flowering. Sowing indoors in late winter is a better option, to grow in a moist, shady spot.

Growing

Big harvests come from growing the plants under cover through winter (see Chapter 19, page 238). For outdoor growing, autumn harvests are assured, and in winter chervil stands temperatures as low as -8°C (18°F). Keep chervil's soil and compost moist; it enjoys shade in summer weather.

Harvesting

Keep picking larger bottom leaves or cut out sections of a multi-sown clump. 'Clear cutting' across the top of plants about an inch above soil level will result in harvestable new growth in two to four weeks.

Chives and garlic chives (perennial)

These plants make perennial clumps of thin leaves that respond well to frequent harvests, either cutting or picking a few leaves at a time.

Sowing

Spring sowing works best, four seeds per module or small pot. Most springs thereafter you should have one or more established clumps and no need to resow.

Growing

When clumps are two years or older, they benefit from being divided in two or three with a sharp trowel, the root that is cut out being replanted in another pot or spot.

Harvesting

Chives are one of the first spring herbs. They even produce their first spiky, onion-flavoured leaves before the start of spring, and they can be repeatedly cut or picked.

By May there will be several stalks of pretty mauve flowers. Eat these after breaking them into small, tasty florets, and then any unused ones are best deadheaded so that seeds do not shed everywhere. After removing all flower

Chervil at the foot of a plum tree in December.

stems in early summer, more leaves will regrow for three to four months, but diminishing in quantity and quality by autumn.

Garlic chives produce flatter, garlic-flavoured leaves, which can be cut from April to late autumn, and delicate heads of white flowers in August. As with chives, the flowers are best either eaten or removed after flowering, as seedlings can be invasive.

Coriander (hardy annual)

Sowing

Sow as for dill below. These herbs need frequent sowing because they tend to flower after making relatively few leaves, except when sown in late summer to early autumn. First sowings in March will yield leaves by early May for about a month, depending on variety.

A coriander called *Cruiser* is slower to flower, has lovely large leaves and is also extremely hardy. Sow in late July for autumn cropping outside, and in late August for winter harvests indoors.

Harvesting

Frequent picking prolongs the harvest, and flowering can also be delayed by repeatedly picking off flower stalks.

If coriander flowers are left alone, you can soon eat the green seed pods. If left to ripen, they turn brown and become hard towards the end of summer. They can then be harvested for resowing and also to cook, although it's a fiddly job to shell the seeds. After picking out the debris, you can blow off the small bits of dust.

Dill (annual)

The strong aniseed flavour of dill is not to everybody's liking but it certainly carries an evocative suggestion of spring, with a refreshing aroma as much as taste. It's a cool-season plant (though not too frosty) if you want long periods of harvest, but grows in summer too.

Sowing

Sow from February until July; early sowings crop for longest, so a second sowing in May, third in June and fourth in late July will provide dill from May to October. Sow three to five seeds in a module or small pot, or prick out seedlings from trays. Any fallen seeds from previous years may well pop up unexpectedly and mean that you always have a plant or two.

Harvesting

Pick whole leaves or some of their feathery tips and you can eat the flower buds too. Plants grow up to 60cm (2') high, and once flowers start to appear in earnest, they are best removed. For collecting seed, you need five or six plants to ensure cross-pollination, as with coriander.

Lovage (perennial)

Rich flavours of celery come from small amounts of leaf, while lovage seedlings are delicious and milder.

Sowing

Sow in spring or autumn in a small pot for planting out. It's easier and quicker to buy a plant or beg some root from a friend who might be dividing a large clump.

Harvesting

Harvest at any time from early spring to late autumn; lovage is vigorous and will grow both tall and wide. Pinch or cut off the flowering stalks in summer.

Mint (perennial)

Occasionally useful in salads, in tiny quantities and chopped into small pieces. Flavours range from fruity apple mint to spicy spearmint.

Sowing and growing

Mint grows readily from small lengths of root and once established will colonize an increasingly large area, to the detriment of any less vigorous plants it encounters. So buying a plant or asking for a piece of root from a friend is easier than sowing, and mint is best confined to pots and containers rather than being allowed to spread through beds and borders.

Coriander *Cruiser* and dill *Delight* in May.

Another option is to grow it in cracks between wall and a stone or concrete path. I do this at Homeacres where a clump of apple mint is just outside the back door, rooting through a crevice and into soil under the concrete path. We need only to open the door for harvests over several months, for herb tea as well.

Harvesting

Keep pinching off the tender growing points of new stems, and remove flowers for as long as you want to keep harvesting. Cut all dead stems back to near soil level at year's end to make picking easier in spring. Tasty new shoots appear as soon as the weather warms up, even in late winter.

Parcel (biennial)

Of strong, metallic flavour, similar to the celery it is descended from. Used raw, a tiny amount of leaves is needed. Grow as for parsley below.

Parsley (biennial)

Perhaps the most worthwhile herb to grow, of many flavours and reliable, steady growth.

Sowing

Two sowings in March and July should supply leaves for more than a year, although there will be few new ones in winter, when plants lie mostly dormant. Seed germinates slowly, taking up to three weeks, and should be less than two years old for best results. But you need so few plants: three or four in a 30cm (12") pot, kept watered, should suffice. Sow four to six seeds in small pots or modules, or prick out individual plants from a seed tray into modules.

Harvesting

Parsley can be cut, but such violence is not normally necessary and large leaves are quite easy to keep pinching out, near to the base of plants, to make subsequent picks easier. If in summer you have too many leaves and some are developing brown spots and yellow edges, it can be worth cutting all of them about 5cm (2") above soil level, to encourage healthy new growth within a couple of weeks.

Problems

All parsley is susceptible to aphids and to carrot root fly, both having the effect of turning leaves yellow and sometimes eventually killing plants. Aphid damage is from the motley dwarf virus they carry, most common in spring. Any plants that suddenly grow bright yellow leaves are best removed to compost.

Root flies are more common in autumn and result in stunted growth. There is also septoria, a leaf disease of damp leaves in autumn; older plants are more susceptible so a July sowing is highly worthwhile.

Varieties

There are two main types, curly and flat-leaved. The curly grows more slowly and is often more hardy and long-lived. Flat parsley tends to flower by midsummer from a March sowing but it has a sweeter and more delicate flavour: for big harvests and large leaves, grow *Giant of Italy*.

Salad burnet (perennial)

Sowing

Sow any time from April to July and I recommend just one plant for occasional leaves as its flavour, or rather its lack of flavour, is not the best. Its leaves are also a little tough and chewy. However, it's easy to grow!

Harvesting

Plants grow large and offer plenty of leaves; pick them as young and small as possible. They produce small, fluffy, crimson flowers. More plants can be created from root division.

Sorrel (perennial)

Is sorrel a herb or a vegetable? It has the strong flavour of a herb, and grows as fast as some vegetables. Broad-leaved sorrel is especially productive: its long, thin, pale green leaves look like spinach yet taste like freshly squeezed lemon juice. All the sorrels have a powerful, citrusy bite and work in small quantities to enrich bowls of plainer-tasting leaves. They are good in omlettes, soups and sauces, too.

Sowing

Sow from March until June; the early sowing can sometimes last through a

Plants are smaller close to the purple sprouting broccoli in a dry spring.

SORREL VARIETIES

There are three main varieties, available as seed or plants:

* Broad-leaved sorrel, which is the easiest to look after and re-grows readily from 'clear-cutting' with a knife.
* Blood-veined sorrel which has strikingly veined leaves are much smaller than broad-leaved; suffers fungal damage in damp weather and has a tannic, dry flavour.
* Buckler-leaved sorrel, which has tiny, tender round leaves that can be shaved off in clumps. It is harder to pick than the other two, especially when flowering on tough little stems that can become mixed up with leaves in picking, but the flavour is superb.

whole year if it is not too hot and dry, especially if the dock beetles stay away. Sorrel is perennial and makes an expanding, long-lived root which offers tender leaves as early as February in mild winters. I also sow new sorrel every year, as young plants have more vigour through the summer. I sow in August for plants to overwinter indoors, in a pot or the ground: the fresh lemon flavour is especially welcome in winter.

Problems

Slugs eat sorrel leaves, and so do the larvae of dock beetles, which are attractively bright and blue-green. They lay clusters of bright yellow eggs on the undersides of leaves, quickly hatching out into hungry babies that make hundreds of holes on nearly all leaves. Three solutions are: to grow sorrel in raised beds or pots, where beetles seem less inclined to go; to harvest all leaves at one time, 1-2cm (½") above the ground, so that the beetles' cycle of growth is broken; and to water frequently, as beetles dislike wet conditions, and sorrel loves moisture.

Sweet cicely (perennial)

Of all the perennial herbs, sweet cicely offers the mildest flavour and the most tender leaves, as much juicy as they are herby, so it can be a larger component in bowls of salad.

Sowing

Seed is a little difficult to germinate, whereas small pieces of root can be cut off in winter and grown under cover in small pots for planting in spring, in beds or in a larger pot.

Harvesting

Keep picking new leaves from mid-spring until late summer, when flowering means less leaf production, especially in dry seasons. Plants grow large if given space or in pots up to 30cm (12") diameter.

FLOWERS

More garden flowers are edible than we realize and I describe a few below. Nearly all herb *flowers* are tasty as well, including most of those mentioned above – chives, garlic chives, coriander and dill especially. I have also eaten chervil, fennel, marjoram and sage flowers, and suspect that all herb flowers are fine to eat, if you enjoy the flavour of the herb leaves. There are also some lovely colours to play with, in the flowers of marjoram and sage for example.

Here is a small selection of the possible ornamental edibles, to which you may add others that you come to like:

Borage (hardy annual)

Easy to grow from seed; so easy that gardens can fill with it if seedlings are not hoed off sometimes. But the gorgeous bright blue flowers, which taste mildly of cucumber adorn almost any food and drink, and are continuously produced in summer from sowings in spring. A white strain of borage is equally prolific, but its flowers are less scintillating.

Sowing

All spring and summer, from March to late July: simply scattering a few seeds is as effective as any other method.

Harvesting

Harvest flowers as soon as they appear; and even with regular picking there will almost certainly be some that set seed to ensure another generation of plants, usually during the next wet, warm spell of weather or the following spring, whichever comes first.

Cowslip

Easy to grow, the fragrant yellow flowers of cowslip offer a mild flavour at a time of year when salad is scarce.

Sowing

Sow from May to July, direct or in small pots for planting out.

Harvesting

Harvest flowers the following spring and leave some to set seed: cowslip can be quite invasive in time, as it grows readily from its own seed.

Heartsease (Viola; hardy annual)

Another easy-to-grow plant that is much smaller than borage. It even hides in cracks and crevices, thriving on poor soil.

Heartsease flowers are beautiful and edible.

Sowing

Sow at almost any time; once some plants have flowered and shed seed you probably won't need to sow again.

Harvesting

Harvest over a long period and enjoy the flowers for eating and decorating.

Lavatera (also called Mallow; hardy annual)

An easy-to-grow plant with mauve and white striped flowers, or variations thereof.

Sowing

Any time from March to July; plants sometimes survive through mild winters.

Harvesting

Flowering is prolific from about June to October. Cut off long stems towards the end of summer, to encourage new growth in autumn and reduce the seed numbers falling.

Marigold (hardy annual)

Calendula Officinalis, of all the many different marigolds, is the most commonly eaten flower. It is also known as English or pot marigold.

Sowing

Sow from March to August for bright orange flowers, whose petals above all are nice to eat. It is another vigorous self-seeder so resowing will probably be unnecessary.

Harvesting

You can harvest flowers all summer, except in hot, dry weather, when plants sometimes go dormant. Deadheading old flowers makes new ones more likely.

Nasturtium (half-hardy annual)

There is a whole world of nasturtiums to play with. Flowers of many and varied hues are edible; likewise the leaves, which range from dark red-green (*Empress of India*) to pale green speckled with white flakes (*Alaska*).

Sowing

Sow in early May – no earlier because nasturtium is killed by frost. Seed can be sown as late as September, when self-sown nasturtiums often appear during the first rains at the end of hot summers.

Harvesting

Harvest flowers and leaves all through summer if it is not too dry. Some are always missed and set seed for the autumn or following year. Cabbage white butterflies lay their eggs on nasturtium leaves, often in preference to cabbage and broccoli leaves, and plants can be stripped bare by the caterpillars. Perhaps nasturtium can be seen as a decoy plant, attracting pests away from brassica vegetables, or perhaps it is just attracting more butterflies into the garden.

Pea (hardy annuals)

Pea flowers have a lovely taste of pea and look fantastic in spring and summer salads. Sow as usual in late winter to mid-spring and harvest a few flowers as soon as they appear, leaving plenty to grow into peas.

Sunflowers (annual)

The petals are delicious, and so are the buds, which are cooked by steaming or boiling; and if you miss those, there are seeds at the end.

Sowing

Sow mid-spring (April, no earlier) under cover, in small pots or modules, and a month later outdoors: sunflowers are killed by frost. Check the seed packet details about eventual size and plant accordingly.

Harvesting

Many sunflower varieties are multi-heading so you can keep harvesting the bits you like. Plants are killed by the first autumn frost, but will sometimes self-seed if birds and mice have missed a few.

Vegetable flowers

Many vegetables do not normally flower, as we eat them before they reach that stage, but all peas, beans, courgettes and squashes are worth a try. Broad bean flowers have a lovely scent and bean-like flavour with some sweet nectar.

Be creative and try some different ones, except for the solanum (nightshade) family.

CHAPTER SEVENTEEN

OUTDOOR WINTER SALADS

DIFFICULT BUT PRECIOUS

Brief summary

* The main sowing months are August and September. Check the details on pages 212-17 for each type of salad.
* Sow in weed-free soil or compost, because growth is slow and weeds often grow more quickly than these salads.
* Expect small harvests.
* Amounts of leaves to pick will vary according to weather.
* Late winter and early spring see a period of relative 'abundance'.
* Flowers that follow this, mostly in April, are edible and tasty.

This chapter explains what can be grown for outdoor leaves in an average British winter. I use the word 'average' because some of what follows will apply neither in a much colder than average winter, nor in a much milder than average winter. Since, at the time of writing, recent winters have varied so much in character and temperature, I am well aware of the uncertainties in planning to grow winter salad, especially outside rather than protected by glass or polythene.

Growing winter leaves outdoors is an inexact science with small and unforeseeable results. However, those results are more precious because of that, and more highly appreciated than 10 times the same number of leaves in summer. I know this is true because why, otherwise, do I go out in bitter weather to hunt for a few leaves of lamb's lettuce? They really matter!

Kale and spinach in the first frost of the winter.

Spinach, mustards and winter purslane in January, netted against rabbits.

Frosted netting over chervil, spinach, mustards and (right) spring onions.

NORMAL PATTERN OF GROWTH

In order to survive and then thrive through winter, salad plants need to be large in root and small in leaf. The root system needs enough reserves to meet the vagaries of cold, storms and frosts. Leaves, on the other hand, are more frost- and weather-hardy when small.

A tricky problem is that one sows seeds in late summer and autumn at a time when the amount of 'growing days' is diminishing fast, and to an unknown degree. Unexpectedly warm weather in September and October can bring plants along too quickly before an unheralded severe frost in November that might weaken or even kill them. Or a cold, wet October might see plants struggling to establish enough before a colder than average winter, when as a result they may scarcely make any significant new growth.

Nonetheless I have been trialling dates for a long time and share them here. They work in a zone 8b (H4 – see Resources) climate and you need to sow earlier if you are colder, later if you are warmer.

After the erratic growth of winter, slow or very slow according to weather, spring sees the same plants making a late surge. You can have a month or two of plentiful leaves until flowering commences.

GROWING UNDER CLOCHES

Cloches are an outdoor alternative to greenhouses and polytunnels, and although they do not match their yields, they work well for winter salad. There is a commitment because they need pulling back if polythene, or taking off if glass for occasional watering and weeding, about once a month between November and March, more in April.

There are an increasing number of proprietary cloches on offer, many of them quite expensive. It is possible to make your own from stiff wire, if you are handy with pliers. My home-made, semicircular hoops have a loop about 15cm (6") above the ends on either side, which go into the soil. So when they are pushed in, on either side of a bed, the loops are just above ground level and string can be passed under (not through) them in a run of one, long string which passes diagonally from the side of one hoop to the other side of the next one.

There are just two knots needed, one at either end. Then tie a string to the loop at the opposite side of an end hoop, and run diagonally along your cloche. In this way the string crosses at right angles to the other string and over the polythene, under the loop of each hoop in turn, until you tie it firm at the other end.

To cover beds at a reasonably sheltered site, here is another way to make a cloche. Cut stout bamboo cane into 20cm (8") pieces and put the pieces firmly in the ground inside each side of your raised beds, at 60cm (2') intervals. Take some rigid but flexible hollow tubing, such as alkathene water pipe, and cut to preferred length, depending on the height of cloche you want and the width of your bed. Fit the tube over the bamboo, making arches across the bed. Cover with either fleece, polythene or netting as required, and secure the cover at either end and either side with bricks or stones.

The best sowing dates in cloches are about a week earlier than those described in Chapter 19, so that plants are well rooted by mid-October. Treat plants similarly and remove slugs when picking leaves, as they quite enjoy cloches.

Covering a bed such as those described in Chapter 3, pages 30-2 should give worthwhile pickings but it certainly involves extra effort to keep everything in order.

FLEECE/ROW COVER

Fleece is prone to rip in winter gales. Plus the weakness of winter sunshine means there is little warmth to trap, so I recommend fleece for spring rather than winter use. In March and April, it can be used very productively to grow extra leaves on existing plants, as well as to bring new plantings into earlier production.

CONTAINER GROWING

Winter salads make an excellent use of beds or containers at a time when they are otherwise not needed. Use the sowing and planting times given to work out how you might slot them in with other salads and vegetables. If preceding crops are not finished before the end of September, you will need to raise plants in pots, trays or modules elsewhere, for setting out plants by early to mid-October.

Some suitable preceding crops are summer lettuce, basil, carrots and French beans. Watering is rarely neces-sary in winter, although slugs can be a problem. I have had best success with rocket, leaf chicories, leaf endives, land cress, winter purslane and chervil.

LAMB'S LETTUCE (also called CORN SALAD)

This intriguing name may originate from the shape of the leaves being similar to lamb's tongues, at a time when people were more acquainted with lambs' tongues than we are now. The other name, corn salad, possibly derives from wild relatives growing in autumn and winter stubble after cereal harvests.

Like most winter leaves, lamb's lettuce makes a small plant that hugs the soil, hence the extra labour involved in its harvest. It has a shallow root system to exploit the continual dampness of soil in winter, and possesses a notable ability to resist frost, considering how tender and juicy the leaves are. They are also slightly waxy, with a buttery succulence that makes a pleasant balance to the fiery taste of rocket and mustard leaves.

Sowing

Any bare soil after summer crops is suitable, as long as it is not too weedy. Chickweed and grasses can quickly swamp slow-growing lamb's lettuce and involve plenty of extra time to control – mostly by hand-weeding in damp soil. Sow directly in shallow drills about 25cm apart with around two seeds per centimetre of drill (10x1"). Seeds are light and blow around, so spacing is rarely exact; also it is often dry at sowing time so germination may happen in stages as soil receives autumn

Mesh supported by cloche hoop over mustards, spinach and salad rocket.

rains. Emergence happens slowly even in ideal conditions, then the tiny seedlings take a long time to get going in warm soil. This even applies to modules in a greenhouse that can be sown until late September. Outdoor sowing for leaves in late autumn and winter is best from mid-August to mid-September. Sowing earlier in the year is possible, say in March for cropping in May, and in July for cropping in September. However, lamb's lettuce does not like hot dry weather which frazzles its shallow roots, so early sowings are extremely weather-dependent: mild, moist conditions are the plants' favourite.

Growing

Once seeds are all germinated, it may be worth thinning seedlings a little because harvesting in winter is a lot easier and more pleasant from a few larger plants than from dense rows of baby leaves.

In a dry September, plants mark time and then put on a spurt when it rains, so watering is often worthwhile for earlier sowings. Keep on top of any weeds, which may otherwise grow over the lamb's lettuce.

Because of its extraordinary winter hardiness, I grow it exclusively outside and there is less benefit in indoor production, compared to other salad plants. Plus lamb's lettuce is prone to mildew when grown indoors (see below).

Problems

The lower leaves are invaded by white powdery mildew in dry weather; and the best remedy if you see it is to water your lamb's lettuce, but plants that are infected take a while to recover.

The risk of mildew is a major reason for not growing lamb's lettuce in late spring and summer. I did once try it and succeeded fantastically, because it was a freakily wet year, just showing how rules are made to be broken as long as you are aware of the risks.

Slugs are much less problematic than for most other salads and, although often present, should confine their attentions to decaying older leaves.

Harvesting leaves

It is a pleasure to watch the tiny rosettes of shiny green leaves enlarge into clumps, but they never grow beyond a certain size, depending on soil and variety. This slows the harvest.

The outer leaves start to yellow at

Even mizuna is slow in winter. This is four weeks after cutting across the top.

about 10 weeks from sowing, at which point the main growth is of new rosettes at soil level, below the older growth above. So it pays to carefully cut the topmost rosette off older leaves, in order to allow more light to the young ones below, taking care not to cut too low, so that new leaf clusters can grow out of the stem is underneath your cut. Secondary and tertiary harvests are smaller until more vigorous growth recommences in late winter, until small buds develop in mid-April with tiny blue flowers soon after. Best remove plants at this stage before they drop seeds.

Varieties

D'Orlanda (also called *D'Olanda*)

This has pale green leaves of a good size and an ability to survive most British winters. I like its worthwhile yield and often space it at 20x7cm (8x3") to allow for the extra growth. Match longer leaves with one for growing in warmer weather.

Verte de Cambrai

Probably the smallest variety, more fiddly to pick but extra hardy and with firm, glossy leaves.

LAND CRESS (also called AMERICAN CRESS)

An extremely hardy plant whose dark green leaves are full of metallic flavour, similar to watercress but, not surprisingly, rather drier in texture.

Sowing

Sowings at any time of year may, in wet years, offer some good leaves before flowering. Otherwise, sow in July and August for autumn and winter harvests, and up to mid-September for picking in winter. Module-sowing works well; space at 22x22cm (8x8"). Seed can be scattered in weed-free soils, or allow plants to self-seed after flowering in spring, although land cress can become invasive.

Growing

Seeds are small so early growth is slow. Although land cress grows a little more quickly than lamb's lettuce and purslane, it still needs careful weeding.

Problems

Land cress is hardy, but leaves are vulnerable to slugs and flea beetles if grown in warmer weather. Pigeons can strip it in cold weather so netting is worthwhile.

Harvesting

Leaves lie close to the ground and can be difficult to gather without lots of soil and compost. Some of the first leaves in autumn are quite large and worth picking individually; thereafter some cutting is easier, a few leaves at a time, but this is also difficult because one tends to cut into the quite long baby leaves at the same time as snipping off the outer leaves. If cuts are made too far from the middle of the plants long pieces of stem are left, which eventually rot and get in

the way of later pickings. Luckily land cress leaves are strongly flavoured enough that you probably will not want to pick many at one time.

New growth in winter is minimal but should resume by mid-March and continue through April, when the flowering stalks can also be eaten; they have a peppery flavour.

Varieties

Apart from ordinary land cress, the only variation I know is variegated land cress, whose leaves are very pretty, mottled with whitish patches; however, they grow more slowly and are fiddly to pick.

MUSTARDS

There is a range of hardy mustards, suitable for salad use. They tolerate temperatures of -5°C (23°F) and sometimes lower, especially when sown in early autumn rather than late summer. You could even sow edible mustards as a 'green manure' on soil otherwise empty in autumn. After being killed by frost, mustards turn into organic matter that is taken in by worms, enriching the soil without any digging. The plants then serve two purposes; food and fertility.

Sowing

Sow as late as mid-September, but late August is more reliable. Fast germination makes mustard easy to sow direct, in rows 25cm (10") apart, with 7-10cm (3-4") between plants. Or 3-4 seeds per module to plant at 22cm (9") after four weeks at most.

Late-winter view of salads and spring onions, sown in autumn.

Growing

Fast growth means you may have some picks in autumn; remove lower, yellowing leaves to compost.

Problems

Brassica pests such as flea beetles make little holes even in winter, but damage is less than in spring!

Harvesting

Mustard leaves grow to a fair size even in winter, after which they turn yellow and suffer more pest holes. Allow plants to establish for about two months after sowing, then start picking larger, outer leaves with a knife or thumbnail. If you cut across the top, regrowth is much slower.

Varieties

For outdoor growing in winter, try Green in the Snow, Green Wave and Red Dragon. You can also eat the growing tips of white mustard sown for green manure.

WATERCRESS

Watercress can be grown without running water, especially in winter when soil is so damp, but it can be invasive in autumn especially, when leaf growth is most rapid, and is killed by moderate frost.

Sowing

Best sown as for land cress. Alternatively, place a clump of bought watercress in water or damp soil, where it should root and grow again.

Growing

If you enjoy DIY, you could follow the example of a friend who has achieved several years of watercress in an old sink with a solar-powered fountain to keep the water oxygenated. Some soil or compost is good at the bottom – perhaps enough to fill a quarter of the depth of the sink.

Harvesting

Harvest by either cutting handfuls of stems or pulling individual leaves.

WEEDS

Certain weeds that are common in late winter and early spring are both edible and tasty. Hairy bittercress and shepherd's purse both have leaves rich in sulphur oils, making them bitter and invigorating. Chickweed is all edible, its little white flowers included, but has a dry and unremarkable flavour. Eating these weeds will both fill your plate and clear the garden of their invasive habits, as long as you clear them before any flowers have set seed.

WINTER PURSLANE (also called CLAYTONIA)

The delicious leaves are equally soft, waxy and succulent, round and dark green, but sometimes of variable quality. If grown without protection through a British winter, pickings will be small and occasional before tasty small white flowers in March and April. There is only a short interval between flowering and seeding and winter purslane can be quite invasive, so be wary of leaving it to grow and set seed in April and May.

Cropping under cover is more substantial – see Chapter 19, page 246.

Sowing

Sow in late summer and even into September. For sowing direct in the soil, use the same spacings as lamb's lettuce. Winter purslane also grows well in modules, a pinch of the tiny seeds giving a clump of several plants in each one, to plant out when the first true leaves are just showing at 22x22cm (8x8").

Growing

Growth is quite slow and steady; keep well on top of weeds.

Problems

There are no major pests or diseases to worry about. Slugs like it for habitat more than to eat leaves.

Harvesting

Purslane can be cropped as soon as it is holding a number of leaves, umbrella-style, above and around its slightly mounded core. By this time it may also be sending up a few small flower stems with pretty, miniature white florets.

Leaves and flowers can be harvested individually but take care not to upset the fragile root system; on occasions you may unfortunately detach whole plants from their roots. It is better to cut bundles of leaves with a sharp knife, over the whole rounded top of each plant/clump: a haircut, not too low. This means that baby leaves closer to the middle are left to grow into the next harvest. In midwinter this may take a month or longer, or half that in milder weather.

Harvesting finishes when the increasing number of flowers become tougher-stemmed in early spring.

Varieties

There are no named varieties on offer at the moment.

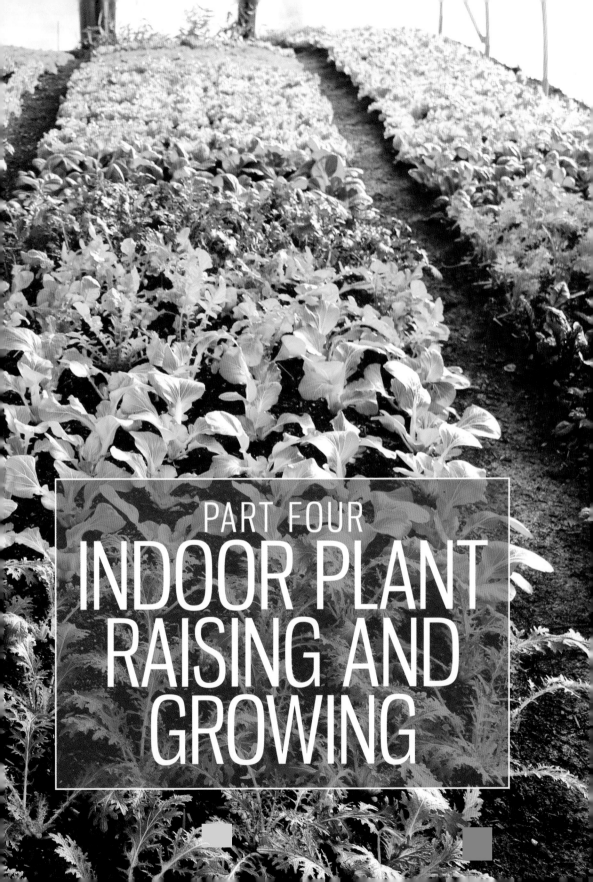

PART FOUR
INDOOR PLANT RAISING AND GROWING

CHAPTER EIGHTEEN

INDOOR PROPAGATION

EARLIER GROWTH, STRONGER PLANTS, MORE HARVESTS

Brief summary

* Sow indoors for more reliable results: less slug and insect damage to seedlings, less weather damage, and earlier crops.
* Use different timings and techniques according to which salad you are propagating.
* Module-raised plants can be used to rapidly establish succeeding crops, and to fill any gaps in existing ones.

A light space sheltered from rain and cold winds makes it possible to raise plants reliably at any time of year, especially in the bright but cool days of spring. It increases the productivity of a garden out of all proportion to its size. Having healthy plants ready to fill gaps at particular times helps to ensures a steady supply of harvests through the year.

Chapter 6 has general details of suitable structures, modules and composts to use. Indoor plant-raising can be fun, but remember that plants need regular water – every day in sunny weather – especially when they are larger and nearly ready to go out. Seed trays need less watering but involve either pricking out their seedlings or thinning them out to grow on. This chapter offers details and plenty of sowing ideas.

Early October module plants for winter salad leaves.

PLANT TRAYS

Most plant trays are made of plastic, and while it is an excellent material for holding compost and moisture, there are also problems of waste and landfill. However, many gardeners do not realize that it is safe to reuse seed and plant module trays and pots without even washing them, and definitely without using disinfectant. All of my seed and module trays have never been cleaned and a few sturdy ones have raised healthy plants for three decades.

So buy the best quality you can find and keep reusing them. Some plastics are now recyclable, but reusing your trays and pots is a greener practice.

Seed and plant trays come mostly in A4 and A5 sizes and can be filled with many different kinds of plants at one time. If you buy plants, they may come in containers that can be reused.

Modules vary in size. Forty to an A4-size tray is good for larger plants and sixty per tray is good for smaller plants – most salads in fact. If possible fill with organic multipurpose compost – see Resources for suppliers.

Plastic module trays are quite cheap and often rather brittle. However, careful use will see them endure a few seasons, although their base may be damaged in pushing plants out. It helps to thoroughly water trays of young plants before planting.

You may also see 'insert trays' for sale. I recommend avoiding these as they seem designed to self-destruct in extracting plants from their flimsy plastic.

Polystyrene trays are more sturdy and roots like them. I have some that are over 20 years old, missing their corners but otherwise working.

Compost needs to be pushed firmly into module trays. Also, when plants'

One month after February's first sowings of spinach, peas and beetroot.

root structures are sufficiently developed that they hold the compost together, rooted plants are quite easy to push out through the holes in their bottoms.

SOWING

Seed trays and module trays can be sown with different seeds at the same time, for eventual planting out together, although different growth rates mean that some may be a little under- or over-mature.

Have a look at the seasonal example of module-sowing on page 224 to gain an idea of what can be sown together.

MAIN MONTHS FOR SOWING INDOORS

The table below is based on the salad seasons and gives a brief outline of the best times to sow different salads with **number of weeks** from sowing to planting out.

	LATE JAN or FEB	MAR	APR	MAY	JUN	JUL	AUG	SEPT
VEGETABLE	WEEKS TO PLANTING							
Basil			9	7	6	5		
Chard		6	5	4	3-4	3-4	3-4	
Chervil						4	4-5	
Chicory				4	3-4	3-4	3-4	
Coriander		6	5	4	3-4	3-4		
Dill		6	5	4	3-4	3-4		
Endive				4	4	3-4	3-4	
Kale						2-3	2-3	
Lamb's lettuce							4	5
Land cress							4	4
Lettuce	6	5	5	4	3-4	3-4	3-4	
Mizuna	5						2-3	2-3
Orache		6	5	5	5			
Oriental leaves						2-3	2-3	2-3
Parsley	9	8	7	6	6	6		
Peas	5	4	3	2-3	2-3			
Radicchio						4	4	
Rocket						2-3	2-3	2-3
Sorrel	7	6	5-6	5	4-5	4		
Spinach	5-6	5	4-5	4	3-4	3-4	3-4	
Spring onions	6-7	5	5	4-5	4	4	4	
Winter purslane							3	4

These numbers are a guideline only. They will vary from year to year and according to the warmth of your propagating facility as well as size of pot or module used.

SOWINGS TO PROVIDE A MIX OF SALAD LEAVES FROM MAY TO NOVEMBER

This programme of sowing is **to provide a daily mix of many different leaves** over at least six months, as long as the plants are regularly picked over and are well looked after. If you want different herbs, choose them from the table of dates on the previous page. The later sowings provide plants to fill gaps after early sowings have finished cropping, for example leaf endive after spinach and radicchio after peas.

February: Lettuce, spinach, peas, parsley, coriander

March: Sorrel, chard, dill, orache

Mid-May: Lettuce, leaf endive and chicory, basil

Early July: Radicchio (or could be late July for smaller hearts)

Late July: Lettuce, hearting endive, spinach, dill, coriander

From early August: Rocket, any of oriental leaves, winter purslane, land cress, chervil

Early September: Rocket, lamb's lettuce (corn salad), mizuna, mustard

FOUR SOWINGS FOR THE FOUR SEASONS

This seasonal example for one or two forty-hole A4-sized module trays is a simpler programme with just four sowings. Seed trays could also be used in the same way, although planting out is then trickier. You can vary the total amounts according to the size of growing area and the module numbers according to your leaf preferences.

Numbers refer to module compartments sown, not seed used – check below to see which salads can be multi-sown. As far as possible, I have grouped fast- and slow-growing plants in the same trays.

For planting out, this number of plants require a growing space of about 3x1m (10x3'). If after planting a few are left over, keep them in reserve to fill any gaps arising from slug damage. With regular picking, they should yield enough leaves for four to six people between May and September, and smaller amounts after that.

March (2 trays)

First tray: 27 leaf lettuce of different varieties, 6 spinach, 3 sorrel, 2 chard, 1 coriander, 1 dill

Second tray: 12 pea, 8 mizuna for a half tray of fast plants; and 14 spring onion, 4 parsley, 2 orache for a half tray of slow plants

Late May (1 tray)

30 leaf lettuce, 3 leaf endive, 3 leaf chicory, 2 chard, 2 dill

Mid-July (1 tray)

24 leaf lettuce, 10 radicchio (for hearting, early and late varieties), 6 frizzy endive

Early August (2 trays)

First tray: 10 rocket, 10 mustards, 10 mizuna or mibuna, 6 kale, 4 pak choi

Second tray: 8 leaf chicory (mixed), 8 spinach, 8 leaf endive, 5 land cress, 5 winter purslane, 4 chervil, 2 chard

SEED RATES AND TIPS FOR MODULE- AND POT-SOWING OF EACH SALAD

Check the chapters on different salads to be clear about which kind you want; for instance, whether it is endive for hearting or for loose leaves. The plan is to grow the number of seedlings in modules that you want in each clump in the ground. No thinning at planting time, although you may if more seeds grow than you wanted.

Amaranth
Fast to germinate in summer warmth, sow a pinch of three to five seeds per module.

Basil *Cinnamon.*

Basil
The most difficult salad plant to raise, needing sufficient heat and not too much moisture when small. Up to five seeds per module should see two to three plants in a clump, while one plant per module results in good pickings over a long season.

Chard
Some chard seeds grow more than one plant and some don't germinate. Therefore, four seeds per module is about right to grow small plants for salad leaves.

Chervil, coriander, dill
All these herbs grow well in a clump so four or five seeds per module is good; if you want larger stems, sow two seeds only.

Chicory for hearting (radicchios)
Reliable germination means that two seeds per module, later reduced to the single strongest seedling, is usually effective.

Chicory for leaves
Sow three to five seeds per module to have plenty of small leaves per clump at picking time.

Endive for hearting
Sow two seeds per module and thin to one seedling after a week or ten days.

Endive for leaves
Individual plants are easiest for repeated pickings of outer leaves. Therefore sow two seeds thinned to one plant.

Kale
Sow up to six seeds per module to have small leaves for cutting. See also page 168 for different sowing options.

Lamb's lettuce (corn salad)
Grows slowly and germination is not

Land cress.

Curly parsley.

always good; try four seeds per module and be patient.

Land cress

Two or three seeds per module, thinned to one, gives plants with larger leaves for easier picking.

Lettuce

Germination is often excellent, so one seed per module can give a 90 per cent success rate. Lettuce also grows well after being pricked out from a seed tray. Cover seed with only a dusting of compost and keep germinating seed sheltered from sun in hot weather.

Orache

Up to six seeds per module or small pot; one such clump should provide plenty of leaves.

Oriental leaves

Most of these grow well from three or four seeds per module, except for Chinese cabbage to make hearts which needs two seeds, later thinned to one plant.

Parsley

Slow to germinate; sow two to five seeds per module, depending on whether you want large or small stalks of parsley.

Peas for shoots

Three or four seeds per module gives a productive clump of pea plants.

Purslane

The seed is tiny; one pinch of four or five per module works well.

Salad rocket

Four or five seeds per module give clumps of plentiful, medium-sized leaves.

Sorrel, broad-leaved

Thickly sown is best for small salad leaves, so about six of the tiny seeds per module is good.

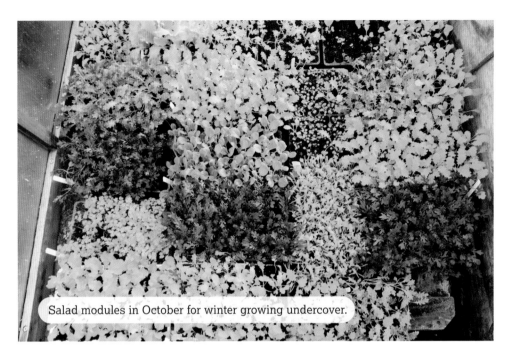

Salad modules in October for winter growing undercover.

August seedlings raised undercover to plant in autumn as other harvests finish.

Planting for winter, after clearing tomatoes and watering thoroughly.

Spinach

Four seeds per module ensures growth of more small leaves, rather than fewer large ones.

Spring onion

You can grow these in clumps of up to eight onions, so ten seeds per module is good practice. Sow deeper than other seeds, under up to 1cm (½") of compost.

HOW BIG A PLANT?

Germination can take a week or two, then seedlings will rapidly grow into small plants. Their size at planting depends on the plant, the season, the compost and on pests in your plot. In other words, there is no absolute right or wrong, and keep your eyes open.

For example, a key signal of plant growth stopping is when their lower leaves – especially the ground-hugging cotyledons – start to turn yellow, indicating that most nutrients in the compost have been used up. How long this takes depends on the compost quality and the plant's speed of growth; experience will help you assess when to expect it. I aim to plant before this happens, to reduce loss of time from growth being checked.

Brassicas are an exception because they toughen up a little as their leaves become less lush and more fibrous. As soon as they look even a little pale, harden them off outside and they will then be fine to plant out.

If over-grown, plants may become diseased. For example, lettuce leaves can pick up mildew on their undersides when they become overcrowded in trays, although this will later disappear after planting out.

WATERING

This simple act is vitally important for successful plant-raising. It is a basic practical task, needing good observation above all. Learn to know the look of dry compost as it cracks away slightly from edges of modules, trays and pots, and to recognize plants that are dry, whose leaves turn a slightly darker colour and become matt rather than shiny.

The opposite problem of over-watering is common on baby seedlings, whose leaves are not transpiring much water and then their stems may rot if over-watering persists. In dull, cool weather you should be watering a third as much as on sunny days. Just keep watching those plants, gradually watering them more as their leaves enlarge.

PESTS

Slugs

Stay vigilant for slugs and snails, because if they are not removed at the first sign of damage, large amounts of potential harvest can quickly disappear. First, clean out whatever structure you are using before sowing, look under any objects lying around and sweep out the dark corners. Then you should be all right for a while, but if ever you notice any eaten leaf, check immediately underneath seed or plant trays, the staging, a crevice in the door frame and anywhere a little damp and sheltered from the sun. The chances are you will find a slug or snail, digesting those leaves and preparing to re-emerge at nightfall.

Woodlice

Woodlice damage young seedlings by nibbling their stems and baby leaves, and they are more difficult to control than slugs because of frequently large numbers. A good sweep out of the propagating area before first sowings is worthwhile, to reduce woodlice habitat.

Mice

Mainly a problem for peas and sweetcorn, as well as cucurbit seeds and sometimes lettuce and spinach. A mousetrap can save you a lot of seeds and time.

Ants

Ants love warm, dry conditions and are difficult to dislodge once established – for example, in the sand of a propagating area. Keeping infested areas moist is the best remedy.

CHAPTER NINETEEN

SALAD LEAVES THROUGH THE WINTER

GROWING INDOORS

Brief summary

* Choose your favoured flavours from the descriptions given.
* Sow mostly in September, plant in October after tomatoes and other summer crops.
* Look after plants with careful and regular picking to keep them producing until spring.
* New leaves are relatively small and scarce in midwinter, more substantial by March and abundant in April.

Not only is winter much enlivened by fresh salad, but some of the prettiest leaves and best flavours grow only in winter months. To expand your range and quantity of leaves, you need a covered space that sees at least half of the available sunlight, to make the most of those precious golden rays.

Overwintered plants then surge ahead in early spring, from March to early May, at a time when few outdoor leaves are ready. Just when some bowls of fresh leaves are most welcome!

Charles dibs holes for planting modules of winter salads in October.

GROWING SPACES

Polytunnels

Tunnels are good for winter salad but are cold at night: growth is usually slow from Christmas to early February. Then in mild springs you may be overwhelmed by the abundance of leaf growth!

Greenhouses

These have greater warmth than tunnels because glass holds more warmth at night than plastic and admits more light, so greenhouses allow more consistent growth. Plants can be grown in a bed of soil with compost added, or on staging in compost-filled containers of any kind, such as old fish or mushroom boxes made of wood or polystyrene.

Aluminium greenhouse frames allow more light than wooden ones. This makes quite a difference in winter.

Conservatories

These are warmer again, but light levels are lower because of house walls, window frames and perhaps a roof. Plants will be longer leaved and thinner; still worthwhile if there is no other option.

CONTAINER GROWING

Containers or pots of salad can be brought into a conservatory or greenhouse in November (see above). Salad plants are happy in any kind of box, tray

Greenhouse salads on 30 December, 10 days after the Christmas pick.

or pot. My website (see Resources) has a video of three mushroom boxes giving 2.3kg (5.1lb) of salad leaves between November and April, in an unheated greenhouse. The boxes had just six plants each.

Larger, deeper containers mean more pickings in the long term, as plants can root more extensively and keep producing healthy leaves over a long period. Come the spring, containers can be moved outside and planted with different kinds of salad; before doing so, it is best to renew some of their compost and reinvigorate the rest – see Chapter 4 pages 41-3.

Space container plants closer than I recommend here, plus you can grow micro and baby leaves through the winter in boxes and trays – again, see Chapter 4.

FLAVOURS

Many winter salads have stronger flavours than summer leaves, making them a good tonic for dark, cold days. Mustard leaves, for example, are hot and peppery.

One of the more frost-resistant salad plants is leaf chicory, although its flavour is bitter. Even so, chicory leaves complement the more fiery mustard leaves, and can be transformed with a sweet dressing to create a lovely balance of bittersweet tastes.

With a little planning and careful picking it is possible to have an extraordinary range of taste in the winter salad bowl. Before sowing, check the information about flavours on pages 235-47 to be sure of having the ones you want.

SEED PACKS

Proprietary seed mixes are worth a try if you are happy to accept a seed company selection. Not knowing exactly what is in there makes growing more difficult, and spending more on labelled seed packets may be better value. I found that salad brassicas, endives and chicories are good for two if not three years of sowing when kept in the spare room. Or you could buy named plants and have an interesting selection – a chance to try just a few different salads.

SOWING
Autumn

Because of rapidly shortening days in autumn, sowing dates are more precise than in spring, when plants of later sowings have more chance to catch up with those sown earlier. During September and October, a week's difference in sowing date will be apparent for a long time, as plants run out of light and warmth. The dates are for southern Britain zone 8b (H4 – see Resources); sow a week earlier in northern Britain.

Winter

If you still have empty gaps in midwinter, they can be filled by sowings after about mid-January if it is not too cold; but it takes far longer than from autumn sowings, for harvestable leaves to grow. Fast-growing brassicas such as leaf radish are good for winter sowing. Early-March sowings of mizuna, pak choi, spinach and leaf endive can also give briefly abundant harvests in April and May.

SPACING

Longevity of harvest is closely linked to distance between plants or clumps of plants: 20-22cm (8-9") allows room for roots to develop over the whole season. Using this spacing also means there will be clear soil around plants, helping to discourage slugs and mildew.

CARE OF SALAD PLANTS IN WINTER

Once established, winter salad plants under cover, correctly spaced, can produce leaves for five or six months, even more in a few cases. So look after them, mainly by careful picking of leaves on a regular basis – although this may be as little as fortnightly in midwinter. Then by spring they will seem like old friends and repay your conscientious attention with amazing harvests every few days. Watering is much less frequent than in summer, best done weekly or sometimes with three weeks between waterings. This allows surface soil and compost to dry out between watering, so that slugs and mildew have less chance to establish. Water more frequently as winter turns to spring.

HARVESTING LEAVES

As well as regularly picking the leaves you want to eat, have an eye for the health of your plants and keep removing any frost-damaged or diseased leaves. This makes it easier to pick leaves the next time, gives less cover to slugs and yields a further important advantage – they grow better! My experience shows how plants feel better about themselves when kept looking nice, and we feel better too when caring for a healthy-looking growing space. A virtuous circle of gratitude is created, benefiting us and the plants.

AFTER HARVESTING

As winter salad plants rise to flower in the spring, you can follow them with exciting summer crops such as tomatoes, melons and peppers. I recommend these rather than planting more salad, to limit any build-up of pests and diseases.

SOIL CARE

If growing in soil in your greenhouse or polytunnel, there is absolutely no need to dig it at any stage. Spreading 50cm (2") of top-quality compost in May, before planting *summer* crops, can provide sufficient nutrients and soil health for them *and* for winter salads planted in October.

Using this amount of compost, I do not feed summer crops like tomatoes. However, I gave the soil a 15cm (6") dressing of compost in year one, to raise fertility to a high level.

By autumn the compost will have been partly taken in by worms and other soil life. The soil/compost surface will be soft, crumbly and just right for setting out small salad plants.

PROBLEMS

See Chapter 8 for tips on keeping slug numbers down: the golden rules are to check for slugs before and in the first two weeks after planting, remove any weeds, keep some bare space between plants, regularly harvest leaves and keep plants tidy.

Aphids may appear in spring but should not become too numerous if you are watering enough. We always see a few whitefly from about March and they can easily be washed off leaves after picking.

Frost should not damage the plants described here unless it is severe – say -10°C (14°F) or colder. Again, regular picking helps because small leaves resist frost better than large ones.

SEED SAVING

I mention this for lettuce, because it's so simple and achievable. Other salads are more complicated, mainly because you need several plants for cross pollination, so they require a lot of space to grow.

SALAD LEAVES FOR INDOOR GROWING IN WINTER

Chard

Flavour

Not the tastiest leaves, but their gloss and deep colour add quality to the mix. Few plants are needed.

Varieties

Grow the colours you fancy, from ruby

Pea plants *Alderman* in modules, ready to plant under cover.

to pink to yellow to white. Paler colours grow faster, darker colours are accentuated in midwinter.

Sowing

Any time in September, depending on when you want to start picking leaves. Early-September sowings are more productive and start producing by about mid-October.

Module-sowing

Four seeds, thin to four plants.

From roots

In late autumn you can dig up the beet-like part of chard roots, trim off the leaves except small new ones and pot them up to keep growing small leaves under cover through winter. For a similar result, place any spare, large beetroots in a pot, half buried in compost, to grow small, pretty leaves until the plants flower in spring.

Spacing

As close as 10-15cm (4-6") gives small and numerous leaves.

Leaf growth and picking

Chard survives frost well by turning a deeper colour in cold weather, losing some of the bright green between its veins. Keep pinching off the outer, dark leaves to eat, then in February and March they become greener and more frequent, larger and fleshier. By late April or early May, plants will show signs of flowering, but can be kept going if you pinch out the tops of any stems. New small leaves then appear lower down on these stalks, but the flavour is more bitter.

Chicory

Flavour

Rather bitter, less so in cold weather.

Varieties

For the range of leaf shapes and colours, see Chapter 12, pages 147-50. Varieties that are easier to pick include *Catalogna Gigante di Chioggia* with long, green leaves and *Red ribbed Dandelion*, of similar habit but with an attractive dark red stalk.

Sowing

September to early October.

Module-sowing

Four seeds is plenty.

Spacing

Standard 22cm (9").

Leaf growth and picking

Stems of the longer-stalked varieties can be repeatedly twisted off or pinched out near soil level as they grow to the size you want. If you cut across the top of plants, regrowth will take longer. By April you may have too many leaves, so repeated cutting is then worthwhile. Flowering stems appear by late April and picking or cutting them out prolongs leaf growth.

Endive

Flavour

Only slightly bitter in cold weather; plenty of 'green' taste because endive is well adapted to grow in low light.

Mustards rising to flower in April; more harvests are possible.

Varieties

A leaf endive such as *Riccia Romanesca da Taglio* (also known as *Romanesco*) grows longer leaves that are easier to pick, though more bitter in flavour. Scarole and frizzy endives (see Chapter 12, page 144-7 for varietal detail) can be grown and picked as for leaf lettuce but are best not allowed to heart up, as they are then more vulnerable to frost, until March at least. *Aery F1* is my favourite for decent-sized leaves in midwinter. *Bianca Riccia da Taglio* has a pretty yellow colour and mild flavour, but is slow-growing in low light.

Sowing

September

Module-sowing

Two seeds, thinned to one plant.

Spacing

Standard 22cm (9").

Leaf growth and picking

Picking small leaves between November and February is fiddly, because leaves lie close to the soil. If you persevere and keep plants tidy, removing any rotten leaves after hard frosts, there should be lovely new growth in March, April and into May. Regular picking in these months will delay flowering, and spring endive plants have an especially vibrant colour.

Herbs

Flavours

A range of possibilities, from the pungency of coriander to the spiciness of chervil.

Types

Flat- and curly-leaved parsley, coriander and chervil are three main possibilities; all resist frost and grow vigorously in March and April. I suggest *Giant of Italy* parsley, *Cruiser* coriander and *Plain* chervil. Dill works in mild winters, anywhere that temperatures stay above about -2°C (28°F), try *Delight*.

Sowing

July or August for slower-growing parsley, August or September for chervil and coriander.

Module-sowing

Between one and four seeds, depending on whether you want smaller or larger stalks.

Spacing

22-25cm (up to 10") allows room for plentiful leaves.

Leaf growth and picking

Much depends on the winter, and coriander may succumb to severe frost, but chervil should keep producing small stems. By March there will be a noticeable difference as plants enlarge and leaves take on a dark, healthy lustre, so keep picking to encourage healthy new growth. Flowering occurs from sometime in early April and is postponed by continual picking of flower stems.

Komatsuna (also called Japanese mustard spinach)

Flavour

Younger leaves are especially mild, while there is more turnip flavour and some pepper in older leaves. All are tender.

Varieties

Usually offered in Britain as 'komatsuna', there is also *Te-Soto F1* for extra vigour and *Red Komatsuna*.

Sowing

Mid-September to early October.

Module-sowing

Four or five seeds per module.

Spacing

Standard 22cm (9").

Leaf growth and picking

One of the fastest-growing vegetables, hence its mild flavour, but it's also seriously prone to slug damage, similar in that sense to pak choi and tatsoi. It resists low temperatures well. Keep picking unless you want large leaves for stir-fries, while the flowers in early spring are tasty raw or lightly cooked.

Land cress

Flavour

Strong, bitter, somewhat acid – best diluted with milder leaves.

Varieties

Ordinary land cress has peppery, dark green leaves; variegated is prettily white in patches, though more bitter in flavour.

Sowing

Late August to September; seed is small and quite slow to grow initially.

Module-sowing

A pinch of seed – one plant is easiest for picking outer leaves, two or three for cutting.

Spacing

Standard 22cm (9").

Leaf growth and picking

Leaves on young plants, especially in midwinter, lie flat to the soil; a little tricky to twist off using a sideways rotation while pulling gently. By early March there is stronger growth and leaves become a little more upright, and then are numerous by April, when stems with small yellow flowers appear. These can be eaten (in small amounts!), and removing them encourages more leaf growth, especially of the variegated cress, which I have managed to keep going all summer.

Leaf radish

Flavour

Just a mild hint of radish in large, tender, deeply lobed leaves.

Varieties

Green leaves can be grown from daikon (mooli radish) varieties, and grow *Rioja* or *Sangria* for red stems and veins.

Late-April salads and garlic in the polytunnel; it's frosty outside.

Sowing

From mid-September to mid October; it can also be sown in January and February but then crops for a shorter time before flowering in April.

Module-sowing

Three to five seeds, large and quick to germinate.

Spacing

Standard 22cm (9").

Leaf growth and picking

Growth is rapid; even the cotyledons are large and worth eating. Regular picking, by cutting or preferably pinching off individual leaves (always being careful not to uproot the plant) prolongs growth until mid-April, when flowering happens quite quickly. Green leaf radish has white flowers; red-stemmed varieties grow pink ones and are really attractive. The radish root may look tempting to eat by early spring, but is usually quite tough.

Lettuce

Flavour

Pleasantly mild, especially by comparison with most other winter leaves. In my cool-season mix I aim for about one third lettuce.

Varieties

We treat *Grenoble Red* as a leaf lettuce and find it the most hardy and long-lived; it also has some slug- and mildew resistance. *Marvel of Four Seasons* and *Winter Density* are two other possibilities, but with less resistance to frost and mildew.

Sowing

September is best, and before mid-month.

Module-sowing

Two per module, thinned to the strongest plant after three or four weeks. Or prick out from a seed tray.

Spacing

Standard 22cm (9").

Leaf growth and picking

First harvests in November may be large but new leaves in winter are tender and usually small. Keep picking them because they can never grow big at that time of year, when there is not enough light. However, from late February you are amply rewarded with larger, firmer and more easily picked leaves. Regular harvesting and correct watering will see robust growth until as late as mid-June for *Grenoble Red*, by which time each plant can have produced over a hundred leaves.

Growing and saving seed

Lettuce is an easy vegetable for saving seed because you need only one plant. Select a good one in March and stop picking, so that it grows large and then hearts up by early summer. Soon after you will see a flower stalk erupt upwards from the heart, and by mid- to late summer (early August in Somerset) you can uproot the plant to rub out its small clumps of seeds. I find that home-saved seed germinates and grows with great vigour.

Steph starts picking outer leaves 23 February, the seventh harvest since November.

Mibuna

Flavour

Long, thin, elegant leaves are a little spicy but not too strong.

Varieties

Normally offered as 'mibuna'.

Sowing

Mid- to late September.

Module-sowing

Average four seeds per module.

Spacing

Standard 22cm (9").

Leaf growth and picking

Lots of thin leaves make it tempting to cut across the top of plants, although patient picking of larger leaves gives more harvests over a longer period.

Mizuna

Flavour

Long, tender leaves are mildly pungent.

Varieties

Not many to choose from; *Kyoto* is reliable.

Sowing

September for leaves before the new year, October for leaves afterwards.

Module-sowing

Three or four seeds per module.

Spacing

Standard 22cm (9").

Leaf growth and picking

Mizuna grows extremely rapidly so needs picking quite soon after planting, unless you want large, long leaves.

Red Frills mustard.

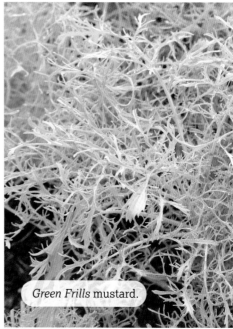

Green Frills mustard.

The latter are more prone to damage by hard frost. Although larger leaves can be regularly picked off, cutting is easier and then regrowth should be harvestable after another three or four weeks. Towards winter's end, flowering stems will appear and they are delicious too. Mizuna's speed of growth counts against it in the stakes for longevity, three cuts is my maximum and the later ones are thinner. However, with one plant per module, I have managed to pick outer leaves for a whole winter before flowering in early spring.

Mustard

Flavour

Peppery yet with a hint of sweetness, and a hot aftertaste of horse radish.

Varieties

Four main ones are *Golden Streaks / Green Frills* for light green, feathery leaves; *Red Frills* (*Ruby Streaks, Red Lace*) for longer and even more indented leaves whose colour darkens to deep ruby in cold weather; *Red Dragon* for fleshy and indented leaves that rapidly grow large if allowed to; and *Green in the Snow* for more compact, hardy and hot leaves. Other varieties include *Red Giant* and *Osaka Purple*, suitable for leaves to stir fry, and *Green Wave*, which is similar to *Green in the Snow* but with wavy leaves.

Sowing

Mid-September to early October, depending on when you want to start picking.

Module-sowing

About four seeds produces nice clumps and gives medium rather then large leaves.

Spacing

Standard 22cm (9").

Leaf growth and picking

Large outer leaves can be individually picked from November to April and mustards can be prolific in mild winters. If it's frosty, there is some damage to stems and smaller leaves cope better. March is the month of abundance and you need to pick more frequently, or eat leaves in stir fries, then flowering happens through April, and new leaves are small again. It is best to remove plants by late April.

Pak choi

Flavour

One of the mildest brassicas and with a crunch to its white stem.

Varieties

Joi Choi F1 is probably the hardiest for overwintering. Red Choi F1 has great colour.

Sowing

Mid-September gives time for plants to establish yet stay youthful enough to resist hard frosts.

Module-sowing

Four or five seeds give a clump of plants whose leaves are not too large.

December salads regrowing after the first pick of winter.

Spacing

Standard 22cm (9").

Leaf growth and picking

Keep picking regularly, unless you want larger leaves for stir-fries, although growth is slow in midwinter. Plants are fragile, shallow-rooted and need careful handling – sometimes I cut leaves individually, to disturb roots less. By mid-April there will be the first flower stems, which are nice to eat, and a diminishing number of leaves. Slug holes are common and we often remove small grey slugs, which hide in the heart leaves; they arrive from nowhere when you grow pak choi.

Pea shoots

Flavour

A pea taste of summer, in winter.

Types

Tall-growing peas make longer shoots but are a little less hardy than dwarf first-early types. Tall peas should grow indoors from a late-autumn sowing if winter is not too frosty; otherwise sow in the new year.

Sowing

Time of sowing depends on variety, location and weather. Early November is possible or, for example, sow tall sugar peas on a windowsill in January for planting in February; there is room to experiment with other dates and varieties. Set mousetraps in outdoor spaces with germinating pea seeds.

Module-sowing

Three seeds per module.

Spacing

22-25cm (9-10") allows sufficient room for harvests over three months.

Leaf growth and picking

Pinch out about 3-5cm (1-2") of the main stem when plants are 25-30cm (10-12") high, or half that for small varieties. For a while afterwards they will stop growing, but new shoots will appear from both top and bottom of the existing and still-growing stem. Keep picking these increasingly plentiful shoots through late winter and spring, even with their flowers on – which taste delicious too. Shoots keep cropping until late June if you keep picking them, and a few peas are possible too from shoots that were missed.

Rocket

Flavour

Spicy with a hot aftertaste, especially the larger leaves and those of older plants.

Varieties

Salad rocket has lobed and fleshy leaves; wild rocket has thinner, denser ones. *Apollo* is a larger-leaved, less-lobed salad rocket, *Athena* is a prolific wild rocket.

Sowing

Mid- to late September.

Regrowth of leaves on a six-month-old salad rocket.

Module-sowing

Three or four seeds per module.

Spacing

Standard 22cm (9").

Leaf growth and picking

For salad rocket, early leaves are the largest; some growth continues steadily through all except the coldest winters and careful picking allows more development of new leaves. Some leaves suffer fungal damage in midwinter and should be removed. By late March you will have plenty to harvest, then flowering reduces yield in April; remove plants by early May.

For wild rocket, growth is slow in autumn and harvests small, to the point that I now grow it in 5-7cm (2-3") pots in the greenhouse, until planting in late winter. Harvests then happen all spring and cutting is possible every two to three weeks until June or even July. Cutting flowering stems extends the season of harvest.

Spinach

Flavour

A welcome change to the brassicas, and it becomes sweeter during and just after cold weather – a real treat in February and March; occasional leaves taste literally sugary.

Varieties

Medania, is the most reliable for resisting frost and has a lovely dark green colour and soft texture. *Galaxy* grows more upright with thinner leaves, while *Red Kitten* has pretty pale red stems and smaller, arrow-shaped leaves.

Sowing

Late August is possible, early September is good too, giving more time for plants to establish. Earlier planting makes it more likely that spinach will outgrow any grazing by slugs and woodlice. If you have used woody composts, you may notice serrations on leaf edges, caused by woodlice. They rarely kill plants but make them unattractive.

Module-sowing

Three or four seeds per module.

Spacing

Standard 22cm (9").

Leaf growth and picking

Keep picking all larger leaves and remove any that are damaged by slugs and woodlice. The latter can stunt growth until plants grow away from them in late winter. Small winter leaves become much larger and fleshier by March and you may then have enough to let some grow into cooking spinach by April. Flowering of *Medania* is later than other salads, by mid-May or later.

Tatsoi

Flavour

Similar to pak choi.

Varieties

There is choice here: the ground-hugging types such as *Bok Choy* are harder to pick (more for a one-off cutting), but a hybrid called *Rozetto* is more upright, while *Yukina Savoy* and *Supi* are also larger-leaved and easier – check the small print in any description.

Sowing

Mid-September is best, to have plants established in the ground by mid-October.

Module-sowing

Four seeds on average.

Spacing

Standard 22cm (9").

Leaf growth and picking

Be wary of slugs as tatsoi is one of their favourites, especially when young, but it should grow away from occasional nibbles by mid-November. Leaves are best cut gently with a knife or pinched off carefully, as the root system is fragile and its leaf stems are firm. Growth is usually good in February and March, often ahead of other salads, but so is flowering – often by late March, and growth finishes in early April.

Winter purslane (claytonia)

Flavour

Tender round leaves have a soft, delicate flavour and texture.

Varieties

Just the the generic winter purslane.

Sowing

September.

Cutting winter purslane under cover in February.

Module-sowing

A tiny pinch of the minuscule seeds usually gives a fine clump of leaves.

Spacing

Standard 22cm (9").

Leaf growth and picking

In a mild winter, growth will be prolific. Cut stems when they are 5cm (2") long and are holding large leaves above new growth at the centre of the clump, from which should come successive cuts at two- to four-week intervals. Cutting the larger leaves around plants' edges, rather than across the top, is less traumatic for them and ensures more rapid regrowth, with significant amounts of leaves from each clump, over the season as a whole. By March there will be some pretty white flowers on their own stems. Soon after you will start to see delicious white flowers on leaves as well – two weeks of fantastically beautiful harvests before the final seeding and smaller leaves of late April. Twist out plants by early May, before they drop seeds.

Other leaves

Next winter I look forward to trying a few different leaves, such as watercress, which I feel may be easier to harvest than land cress. I shall also be sowing some Chinese cabbage in mid- to late September, for growing as a leaf plant to keep picking, as I have a feeling it could be one of the most productive winter salads of all – as long as I can keep the slugs at bay!

RESOURCES

BOOKS

Back Garden Seed Saving: Keeping our vegetable heritage alive
Sue Stickland. eco-logic books, 2008.
Concise advice on how to save seeds in the garden from many common vegetables.

Creating a Forest Garden: Working with nature to grow edible crops
Martin Crawford. Green Books, 2010.
A huge range of useful information, looking at the principles of forest gardening. Wealth of detail.

Gardening and Planting by the Moon
Nick Kollerstrom. Published annually by Quantum.
People who garden by the phases of the moon believe that its gravitational pull on the earth's water has a bearing on plant growth.

Gardening Myths and Misconceptions
Charles Dowding. Green Books.
Aimed at saving the reader's time and money, explaining the labour- and resource-demanding misunderstandings which are still common among gardeners.

Grow Your Own Vegetables
Joy Larkcom. Frances Lincoln.
Practical; to the point; authoritatively written by a veg-growing legend.

Hot Beds: How to grow early crops using an age-old technique
Jack First. Green Books.
How to make and sow hotbeds for early crops.

How to Grow Perennial Vegetables: Low-maintenance, low-impact gardening
Martin Crawford. Green Books.
Wide-ranging subject matter, lots of good ideas and plenty of information on lesser-known, edible perennials.

How to Grow Winter Vegetables
Charles Dowding. Green Books.
For food all year round, this book actually covers much of the year, from sowing in spring to harvesting in the hungry gap of spring!

Organic Gardening: the Natural No-dig Way
Charles Dowding. Green Books.
Best seller in its third edition, covers most vegetables and some fruit too, with a first part that many readers say is like reading a novel!

Teaming with Microbes: The organic gardener's guide to the soil food web
Jeff Lowenfels and Wayne Lewis. Timber Press, revised edn 2010.
An excellent explanation of soil life, in fact this book brings the subject matter alive too and will enthuse you.

The Biodynamic Sowing and Planting Calendar
Maria Thun. Published annually by Floris Books.
Used by biodynamic gardeners and others to determine auspicious times for sowing, planting and cultivating.

The Moon and the Growth of Plants
L. Kolisko. First published in 1936 and later reprinted by Kolisko Archive Publications, 1978.
A classic biodynamic gardening book.

The One-Straw Revolution
Masanobu Fukuoka. New York Review Books Classics.
Describes the development and impact of the Japanese scientist-farmer's revolutionary natural farming methods.

The Polytunnel Handbook
Andy McKee and Mark Gatter. Green Books.
A manual that covers all aspects of high tunnel or polytunnel ownerÂship, from planning and building to cropping.

The Salad Garden
Joy Larkcom. Frances Lincoln.
A classic original look at many salads we now take for granted.

Viktor Schauberger: A Life of Learning From Nature
Jane Cobbald. Floris Books.
The man who understood water better than anybody.

ORGANIZATIONS

Garden Organic & Heritage Seed Library 🇬🇧
www.gardenorganic.org.uk
A UK campaigning and research charity. The website is full of information on all organic horticultural matters.

Soil Association 🇬🇧
www.soilassociation.org
UKÕs leading membership charity campaigning for healthy, humane and sustainable food, farming and land use.

Royal Horticultural Society (RHS) 🇬🇧
www.rhs.org.uk
Wide ranging advice. Hardiness ratings.

Société Nationale d'Horticulture de France 🇫🇷
www.snhf.org
Advice on growing fruit and veg as well as medicinal plants.

American Horticultural Society (AHS) 🇺🇸 🇨🇦
www.ahs.org
Advice, help and guidance for gardeners in America.

Rodale Institute 🇺🇸 🇨🇦
http://rodaleinstitute.org
Founded by organic pioneer J. I. Rodale, to study the link between healthy soil, healthy food and healthy people.

Royal New Zealand Institute of Horticulture (RNZIH) 🇳🇿 🇳🇿
www.rnzih.org.nz
A great resource of research and best practice.

SUPPLIERS

Chiltern Seeds 🇬🇧
www.chilternseeds.co.uk
Hundreds of salad seedsfor all seasons.

CN Seeds Ltd 🇬🇧
www.cnseeds.co.uk
Salad specialists - unusual seeds.

Delfland Nurseries 🇬🇧
www.organicplants.co.uk
UK's leading commercial organic propagator, certified by the Soil Association.

Ferryman Polytunnels Ltd 🇬🇧
www.ferrymanpolytunnels.co
A range of polytunnels for sale, with installation on request.

Herbary, The 🇬🇧
www.beansandherbs.co.uk
Unusual seeds.

Implementations 🇬🇧
www.implementations.co.uk
Copper tools of high quality.

Jekka's Herb Farm 🇬🇧
www.jekkasherbfarm.com
An outstanding selection of herb seeds and plants.

Mr Fothergills Seed and Plant Catalogue 🇬🇧
www.mr-fothergills.co.uk
Extensive range of quality seeds.

Plants of Distinction Abacus House 🇬🇧
www.plantsofdistinction.co.uk
Interesting and unusual lettuce, chicory and similar seeds for salads.

Primrose 🇬🇧
www.primrose.co.uk
A good value range of accesoires - mesh, fleece, netting etc.

Real Seed Catalogue, The 🇬🇧
www.realseeds.co.uk info@realseeds.co.uk
Unusual varieties and good explanations of how to grow and pick them.

REMIN 🇬🇧
www.reminscotland.com
Basalt rockdust.

Suffolk Herbs 🇬🇧
www.suffolkherbs.com sales@suffolk-herbs.com
Leading UK supplier of seeds and plants for the Grow Your Own Enthusiast.

Thomas Etty Esq 🇬🇧
www.thomasetty.co.uk,
sales@thomasetty.co.uk
Suppliers of heritage seeds.

West Riding Organics 🇬🇧
www.westridingorganics.co.uk
Organic potting compost which includes rock dust.

Franchi/ Seeds of Italy 🇮🇹
www.franchisementi.it;
www.seedsofitaly.com
Especially good for chicory and endive.

B & T World Seeds 🇫🇷
www.b-and-t-world-seeds.com
matthew@b-and-t-world-seeds.com
French compnay supplies seeds from over 5,000 different plant species or varieties.

Graines Baumaux 🇫🇷
www.graines-baumaux.fr
One of the older vegetable seed companiesin France-tomatoes, kales, chicories- you name it, they've got it.

Bingenheim Saatgut AG Organic Seeds 🇩🇪
www.bingenheimersaatgut.de
Sells only open pollinated varieties of organic seeds and plants.

Baker Creek Heirloom Seeds 🇺🇸 🇨🇦
www.rareseeds.com
Tried-and-tested heirloom varieties, all open-pollinated, so you can save your own seed.

Evergreen Seeds 🇺🇸 🇨🇦
www.evergreenseeds.com
A huge collection of articles on plant care, equipment and advice from enthusiasts and experts.

Fedco Seeds 🇺🇸 🇨🇦
www.fedcoseeds.com
This cooperative offers organic seeds and plants and gives workers a real voice in running the company.

Four Season Farm 🇺🇸 🇨🇦
www.fourseasonfarm.com
The experimental organic market garden in Maine, USA, owned by Barbara Damrosch and Eliot Coleman.

J.L. Hudson, Seedsman 🇺🇸 🇨🇦
www.jlhudsonseeds.net
A public access seed bank based in Claifornia, aims to preserve botanical biodiversity and the propagation and dissemination of rare, threatened and endangered plants.

Johnny's Selected Seeds 🇺🇸 🇨🇦
www.johnnyseeds.com
Thousands of varieties, many bred on-site. The website is packed with useful tools, including a seed calculator and growers library.

Kitazawa Seed Co 🇺🇸 🇨🇦
www.kitazawaseed.com
customerservice@kitazawaseed.com
The oldest seed company in America specializing in Asian vegetable seeds.

Richters Herbs 🇺🇸 🇨🇦
www.richters.com
Richters has been growing and selling herbs in Toronto since 1969.

Seeds of Diversity 🇺🇸 🇨🇦
www.seeds.ca mail@seeds.ca
Seed savers who protect Canada's seed biodiversity by growing it and sharing it with others.

Territorial Seed Co 🇺🇸 🇨🇦
info@territorialseed.com www.territorial-seed.com
Organic seed suppliers on a sustainability mission.

The Diggers Club Australia 🇦🇺 🇦🇺
www.diggers.com.au
Heritage and organic vegetable seeds.

WEBSITES

rediscover.co.nz
Blog from New Zealand urban homesteader Julie Crean, with posts on the challenges of self-reliance in a suburban bungalow.

urbanhomestead.org
The tale of the Dervaes family's experiments in self-su_ciency in Pasadena, just 15 minutes' drive from downtown Los Angeles.

www.growfruitandveg.co.uk
The website of Grow Your Own magazine, with lots of good growing articles and a very lively forum.

www.herbnet.com
Encyclopedic US website includes exhaustive details of the habits and uses of every herb you can think of..

www.motherearthnews.com
Among the first and still one of the most popular sustainable lifestyle websites (also
a paper magazine).

www.soilfoodweb.com
Website covering the work of the soil expert Dr Elaine Ingham. Based in the USA, with many online resources and webinars.

INDEX

Page numbers in **bold** indicate a major treatment of a subject: those in *italics* refer to illustrations